ODD MERCY

ALSO BY GERALD STERN

Bread Without Sugar
Leaving Another Kingdom: Selected Poems
Two Long Poems
Lovesick
Paradise Poems
The Red Coal
Lucky Life
Rejoicings

ODD MERCY

Poems

GERALD STERN

W. W. NORTON & COMPANY
New York
London

The text of this book is composed in New Aster
with the display set in Friz Quadrata. Composition
by Crane Typesetting Service, Inc.
Manufacturing by Courier Companies, Inc.
Book design by Charlotte Staub

Library of Congress Cataloging-in-Publication Data
Stern, Gerald, 1925–
        Odd mercy : poems / Gerald Stern.
            p.   cm.
        I. Title.
    PS3569.T3888O83   1995
    811'.54—dc20   95-5390

ISBN 0-393-03879-3

W. W. Norton & Company, Inc.,
500 Fifth Avenue, New York, N.Y. 10110
W. W. Norton & Company Ltd.,
10 Coptic Street, London WC1A 1PU

1 2 3 4 5 6 7 8 9 0

CONTENTS

ACKNOWLEDGMENTS

Some of these poems have been published in the following magazines and journals:

American Poetry Review: "Birthday," "Hinglish," "Hot Dog"
Black Warrior Review: "Diary"
Colorado Review: "Odd Mercy"
Exquisite Corpse: "Love Me," "The Sorrows"
Field: "Only Elegy"
Kenyon Review: "Ida"
The New Yorker: "St. Mark's," "Most of My Life"
Poetry: "Did I Say," "Light," "Mimi"
TriQuarterly: "Blacker than Ever"

"Ducks Are for Our Happiness," "Birthday," and "Bitter Thoughts" were published in the *Bread Loaf Anthology of Nature Poetry*; "The Jew and the Rooster Are One" was published in *Transforming Vision: Writers on Art* (Edward Hirsch, editor); and "Blue" was published in a special collection of poems on painters in the Iowa Museum of Art (Jorie Graham, editor). "Oracle" and "Essay on Rime" appeared in *Cutbank* Spring 1995, along with an interview.

I.

Birthday

It is that they spend so much time in the sky
that bluebirds have streaks of red across their chests;
and it is that—except for the robbing of their houses—
they came north for my birthday bringing the light
of southern Texas with them. Every year
I am able to do the mathematics
and stand like another bird—outside my door—
with one foot in and one foot out, half-looking
for the first light and whisper one phrase or other—
one or the other—and look for a streak of red
and a flash of blue. If you asked me what I lived for
I'd say it was for knowledge; I'd never say
I was waiting to see the sun come up
behind the willow; or I'd say I was living to see
the bluebirds come east again; I'd never say
I was waiting for justice, or I was waiting
for vengeance and recovery; I'd say
I was waiting to see the thumbnail moon
at five o'clock in the evening, or I was waiting
to see what shape it takes by morning or when
it becomes an acorn moon. I'd never say
the bluebird has disappeared from the east, the starling
has driven him out; I'd never turn to the starling
and the English sparrow and hate them for their stubbornness—
how could I as a Jew?—I'd never say
the pigeon is our greatest pest; how could I
who came from New York City myself? I'd say
it's too late to go to Idaho and sight
the distance to the pole; I'd say I'll never
move now to southern Arizona—I'd let
the forest come back to Pennsylvania. I am

half-English when it comes to trees; I live
for the past as much as the future—why should I lie?
I am ruined by the past. I can trace
my eyelids back to central Asia.
                                                    It is
when the thaw comes and the birds begin to swell
with confusion and a few wild seeds take hold
and the light explodes a little I lie down
a second time, either to feel the sun
or hear the house shake from the roar of engines
at the end of my street, the train from North Dakota
carrying sweeteners to Illinois, moving
forward a single foot, then backwards another,
one of those dreary mysteries, hours of shrieking
and banging, endless coupling, the perfect noise
to go with my birthday, grief and grinding enough,
wisdom enough, some lily or other growing
on the right-of-way, some brakeman still wearing a suit
from Oshkosh, he and I singing a union song
from 1920, some dead opossum singing
something about a paw-paw tree, his hands
over his eyes, some bluebird greased with corn oil
and dreaming of New York State singing songs
about the ruins or about the exile, notes
from southern Texas, notes from eastern Poland,
drifting into the roundhouse, Lamentations
of 1992, a soft slurring
on her part, a tender rasping on mine,
though both of us loving the smell of mud, I think,
and both of us willing to snap some twigs, although
for different reasons I think, and both of us loving

light above all else, almost a craving
that occupied our minds in late February
and made us forget the darkness and the wobbling
between two worlds that overwhelmed us only
a month or two before. It has to be
the oldest craving of all, the first mercy.

Odd Mercy

I kick a piece of leather; except for the claw
it's mostly sky. Let the silkweed bury it
and let the silkweed bury the silkweed. There isn't
a particle of life there, that's if leather
can have a life. Silkweed sends its seed
to cover the body—there is grease; there are
feathers on the claw. Juice, I think,
juice of the cat, juice of the silkweed. The pods
are empty, there is no cream, only a little
white left over, dry and fluffy. Let the
nail bury the nail, let the helmet
of someone named Knute bury the helmet of someone
named Si or Cyrus. Inside the bliss is gone,
the mind is empty; it has moved from one form
of grasping to another. I lift it up,
it is a kind of football, something between
a dry tongue and a ball. I execute
a perfect dropkick, claw after claw—there still
are dropkicks in Pennsylvania. It could be
the self growing more aloof that gives me the courage,
something I can hide behind. I still
freeze when I see a corpse, the spiteful dead
imitating the living, still lying there
with a hand between their thighs, or a paw lifted up
against the light. Let the clogged-up neck
bury the clogged-up neck, let the wristbone
bury the wristbone. If there is someone named Si
let there be someone named Cyrus, let him run
like Knute ran. In my thirteenth and fourteenth year
I spent my afternoons at the Schenley Oval
running until it got dark. I was alone

on the ancient track.—Was it a mile and a quarter?—
I know the empty stands were still intact
the way they were when horses rounded the bend.
The palings were even intact. Let the dark boy
with the long face come and stand at the railing, let him
comb his hair, the part on the left, let him
wipe away the sweat, then look at the moon
while he waits for his father; he will spend his lifetime
waiting. If there is a brown seed on his shoulder,
if it came from the plant beside the fence, it is almost
lighter than life and came by air to land
as the current decided. He reaches for a twig
and breaks it off, the pods are perfect, they are
like round canoes with graceful prows and ribbing
that holds the silk together. He had vertigo—
from running, he thought—sometimes he stopped on a sidewalk
or under a tree to feel it—it was the pleasure
he kept to himself. I still have that pleasure. Who is
the football, he or I? Who is the cat?
Am I or he? The "son of man," what is that
in the other writing? He has neither a Sears
nor a Posturepedic. Let me be the father
and bury myself. Follow me. We are
sitting on wooden boxes. We are singing
without lungs! Let the sea horse bury
the sea horse, let him die standing up. The foxes
have condominiums, the birds have silkweed
but my poor son doesn't have a sofa, he
and I are snoring, don't tell a soul. I can't
at my age start a second life, where will I
find another wife—at the airport?—how can I

stand in line for a job, how can I fight
for air again, what if I had to buy
new furniture? There is a cat inside. I love him
for dying. There is a way of kicking a suitcase
in front of the agents, one foot back and onto
the scale, there are tags all over, there are
books inside and underwear, the cat
is in a rage, there is silkweed, it drifts
like insulation over the brushes, it falls
like snow in the farthest pockets, there is toothpaste
and Neutrogena and Solex; there is a clock
I bought in Siena, it is a German clock,
a *Peter*, with three stars and a kind of forties'
face; it ticks like an ancient bomb, the size
is perfect, the paint is a little chipped, it is
a second heart for the cat and after a day
of odd mercy another one for me.

Blue

What I was hunting for was a skeleton key
and an old pack of Luckies wrapped in foil so I
could add to my silver ball. The blue that lasted
lasted for years; in fact the sky at the end
was almost stark, there was no wind, and the clouds
were puffs at the most and in a sort of childish
formation. I did this before, I walked through a mountain,
I climbed some stairs, but this time there was no letup,
I couldn't walk over the brooms, I couldn't get either
under or over a fallen tree, and salt water
almost made me blind. I wanted to match
the blues, it was that simple, I had a kind of
larkspur love. You understand that blue,
even if dark, was my connection; I would have
sworn, if someone asked me, that my blue
was like the other one and all my bitterness
was just the result of some stray degradation,
brooms in this case, a knife or two. Can I mention
my ear was pink? Can I talk about that pink?
But can I say that it was huge and spread
from ear to ear? But can I say it listened
to everything? It was pink and listened
to everything. Though I only needed one cloud
to hide behind, one puff. One puff lifted me—
it sort of sucked me in—and though my leg was
exposed the cloud concealed me. White was my face
and then some, fog was my forest, smoke was all
around me. There I was holding my dress up
with one hand, banging through the roof with the other.
Green was my rotten liver. Blue were my bloodshot eyes.

Bitter Thoughts

I didn't listen to one stone this year
or one drop of water. I climbed my arborvitae
and held on for dear life. My foot was always
too big and here I was in my sixties freeing
one leg again. It was always that. One bush
was reddish brown. I loved the color but hated
the stiffness. One house was blowing such dirty steam
I thought it was my childhood again. The stone

was blue at the base, half from the river, half
from the slate inside. It faced the island. Moss
of some kind grew on top. If it were a mountain
there would be wind, there would be a branch. What was it
that made me moan like that, that made me touch
the vein above my left ear and reduce
the pain through thinking, through *thoughts* to be exact,
bitter thoughts? I was on a train

to be exact, I was going back to New York
from Philadelphia—I was reading Horace;
a fire had started somewhere in the cable
or in the rubber underneath. There was
a little smoke already. We were hurried
forward; the train was rushing through New Jersey
and rocking from the speed. The light was sputtering
and I was reading and rubbing the vein above

my left ear. The pain was leaving. I could feel
it leave. That was yesterday, the end
of January, 1991; today
the sun is out. The train got to New York

and I was in my apartment in twenty minutes,
not one minute more. I sat in my coat
looking out the window, I couldn't see
details, but I only wanted the shape

and nothing more—maybe a little sky
between the top of my window and the roofline.
I notice today, sitting in my bathrobe,
how large the trees are—I had to look through the branches
to see the sky, but I don't remember; one fence,
of all the fences, is made of wood and there is
ivy growing over it, there are flagstones
behind one building and there is a charcoal burner

with last year's charcoal still intact behind
another. Not one goat. I was never
a tree-climber, though more from fear of heights
than from the size of my foot but I was up high enough
to see the river and see the lapping without
hearing it. The island was out of sight
from where I stood—I could have hung from the limb
and seen the tip of it, if I could climb

out of my heavy shoes, if I wasn't frozen
with fear. The stone was one of those stones for thinking.
It had a seat. The hand went up to the chin
naturally. It was surrounded with sand
and there was a stick to help you, some dry twig
lighter than air, something so soft it broke
as soon as you pressed it a little. It was the fire
though that set me thinking, and it was Horace

that set me drifting. There is a poem he wrote
about a trip to Brindisium. I read it
once or twice a month to get the secret.
I worry that I have *created* him, that he is
not that modern, but every time I read it,
although I know it now by heart and *say* it
rather than read it, I want to be sitting there
drinking new red wine with the Roman poets

and turning some skinny thrushes over the fire
rather than sitting by a window alone
in New York City, counting branches. His day,
or so he said, always ended by eating
a little cereal and going to sleep; it was
a good meal for a poet. My day ended,
at least today—yesterday—by racing
into the station at top speed, bypassing

Newark, as I remember. I was standing
between the cars, the plates were turning, we were
hanging on—and coughing—there was something
exhilarating in it; maybe New York
was being delivered; maybe disease was withdrawing
and no one will die untimely, maybe pain
and hatred will be unknown, maybe mosquitoes
will leave their holes and minister to children.

My driver was Haitian; he believed felicity
will cover the earth. He only charged me four dollars
so I had something left for breakfast. The birdbath
I loved the most and the rows of chimneys second,

though nothing surpassed the dead leaves on the trees
or the canvas chairs. I could find the stone,
if I had to, and the tree. The island is drowned
in garbage now; the river is ruined. I put

one orange on a dish, that is a sign; I turn
the lock two times. Just going down into the street
I am revived—I am sweetened. The foreign
and bitter are here. I love them always; but I have to
be alone upstairs. There is a bookcase
lying on the sidewalk; I'll come back
in an hour to pick it up. I know the wood
is almost split; words have ravaged it. Who
could have thrown it out? Next year, next January,

maybe I'll find a harp, or the end of a lute
with a wire attached, maybe the wind will sing
for me—there on a granite curb—and maybe
knowledge will come and I will understand it
once and for all, the light that first existed, the
struggle between imperishables, what I thought of
for most of a life, near a water-stained lampshade
that saved the world and an overcoat that renewed it.

Ducks Are for Our Happiness

For Philip Levine

Ben Franklin again, down by the esplanade
watching the green ducks flapping, eating a bagel
from Bruegger's, sipping his coffee, eating his heart
out again, remembering spring after spring—or was
it love after love. He feels like a fool, in spite of
his letters. He likes the face of the mallard, he finds it
sweet, and quizzical. He loves when the sun shines
directly on the neck; he loves how the mallard
cleans itself; he tries to bend his neck
and rub his beak on the feathers. He is angry
because of his loneliness; he likes the head
going back and forth; he likes the speed. It is
the warmest day yet. If he could sit here an hour
he would be happy. "Ducks are for our happiness,"
he says in a letter to Fresno. "They resolve
our fear of separation." I am reminded
constantly of Sappho, how the heart
in her ribs shook with misery, how her tongue
was broken and her eyes were dead to the light.
"But he is determined," he says to Fresno, "to put
sorrow on the other burner." He is
disgusted with lovers' moping—at his age—
restless thoughts—and slouching—"he who started
with a bun," he says to Fresno, "ends up with a package
of day-old bagels." He tosses a piece of poppyseed
to one thin duck whose head goes back and forth
as if it were on a spring. He spreads cinnamon
among the sleepers. He curses what has happened
to Jewish bread, but then he settles in
to watch the ducks until it gets cold. His river

is narrow now, it once was huge, he barely
could see across—it seemed to rise in the middle—
and when the thaw came there were sometimes trees,
and deer, and sofas, floating by; this river
is more like a small canal, even the bridges
are small here, but he likes how it turns on itself
as if it still were looking for its outlet,
and that's something. He finishes his letter
and brushes the crumbs off. One green duck pursues
him, it is his own voice shrieking; it stands
its ground—like a dog—it is the way that grief
stands its ground; fear and sadness combine
to make him like that. He rubs his own neck raw—
for this is *his* weakness—and dips his bill in water
to try to get his strength back. Franklin, dear Fresno,
tries to pet the duck and ends up running
down the esplanade in reckless pursuit
of his own voice, of a brawling duck
angry beyond belief, moving sideways
into the bushes, sliding into the river
to get away, carrying the anger with him,
cries of irksomeness, agitations, dark
nights of the soul; arranging the transfer to him
of another's unhappiness, the water of misery
he swims in; as Franklin arranges the *Ethics* and studies
the slats on his bench. The ducks would die for him,
if they had to, they are magic. Is it the oil?
Is it the feathers? And how do they know his oddities?
He walks between two bridges talking French
to his youngest sweetheart, he has written her letters
in two languages, she read to him at night

and fixed his pillows. She, of all his loves,
he longs for most; he wants to watch her again
bend her head to the ground as she brushes her hair,
he wants to bring her chocolate, he hates loneliness
and he hates anger disguised as pity. "He could
write about it," he tells the ducks, "dejected
facial expressions, vain imaginations,
even whimpering." The ducks only sing.
My God, that is their singing. "Think of that,"
he tells no one, "think of the ducks singing;
my God, their warbling, their near notes and their far notes;
their low-pitched chucks; their musical trills, their whistles,"
he says to the river. "My God, their happiness, Fresno!"

Diary

I am at last that thing, a stranger in my own life,
completely comfortable getting in or getting out of my own
   Honda,
living from five cardboard boxes, two small grips,
               and two briefcases.

I stopped smoking, I stopped eating eggs,
            I stopped taking elevators.
I am as good sitting on a rock or a piece of concrete
          as I am on a padded lawn chair.
I am starting all over with a marigold, a green tomato,
        and a string of weak-backed
   delphiniums.
I am putting a brown rose to my lips as if the slaughter
         never happened.

I am a blue-moon singer, getting up on the wrong side,
taking refuge from my own bitter candor,
seeing one too many halos and one too many runaway
   crescents
         and one too many cheese-shaped
   candles a month.
I started off mourning, I started off with a long-stringed
   cello
and a pinch-lipped French horn and a flowering spit-cupped
   trombone
and ended up with a piano and a bell and a sliding hand
and a studio falsetto and a block for a horse's clatter.

There is a cement sidewalk between the irises for my stroll
and a wire fence for my concentration.

There is a metal chair to sit on and another one to hold my tea.
I will stay for the radio blast
and the rattle of the Greek newspaper
and the scream of the jay,
and wait all day for the moon behind the chimney
and the moon above the roof,
a mixture of two cold things
in the dark light.

The steps I will take for the most part one at a time,
holding on to the rail with my right hand
and rubbing the chalk away with my left.
I will lie on the other side this time
because of the oak mirror
and drag two heavy blankets over my head
because of the cracked window.
I will choose "Dust, Dust, Dust"
for my first sleep
and "A Kiss to Build a Dream On"
for my second
and be a just man for half of my six hours
and a bastard for the other.

An American crow, a huge croaker, a *corvus*,
who caws four times, then caws five times at six
in the morning will be my thrush,
and I will turn from painted door to hanging spider to crooked
    curtain rod
to hear his song.
Nothing in either Egypt or Crete
could equal the light coming into this room

or the sound of the Greeks shouting
behind their bolted windows.
And nothing ever was—or could be—different
than my lips moving one way
and my hands another
before coming down together
for an early breakfast
and an hour or two of silent reading
before separating in front of the boxwood
and kissing goodbye over the wilted hostas
and holding on between the few late pinched tomatoes
and the whistling dove.

Mimi

For all that grackles are despised
I saw a baby grackle
walking on the red leaves
around my Honda. I chased

her from right to left, she ran
with the speed of a sandpiper, she ran
with the speed of a pigeon. I saw
she was a baby when she lifted

her wings—she looked like a chicken—
and I knew she was young when she turned
to wait for me. I think
she was playing, even when she stopped

to pick at a seed or a crumb,
walking from right to left,
sometimes running when I half
caught up to her, but never

flying away, that would be
the end of our game. I love
all species whose children are the size
of their own mothers, that means

the cowbird, as well as the grackle,
that means the robin. I love
the rose that waits. I love
the tulip gorged with blood,

I love all pigs that live on
the shit of other animals.

I love the cardinal who spends
her life with the bluejay. I love

the hatred between them. There is
a black-and-white cat who chases
my squirrels; I love how she climbs
my arborvitae and drops

on the roof outside my bedroom.
I love her grief as I lift
my window to let her in.
Did I say the squirrel baited her?

What would I do if the grackle
stopped running? There was a pigeon
in Rome who refused to move;
I think she was dying, her eye

was lifeless, I was afraid
to touch her. The eye of the grackle
is like a flame, her heart
beats four hundred times a minute.

I stuff my pocket with leaves.
What should I do? They sometimes
are wet one day, then dry
another. Some are so huge

they cover my plate. I'm listening
to *La Bohème*. It gives me
a second history. My grandfather
heard it in Poland. Puccini

was more a hawk than a grackle;
he hunted larks. His singers
were scattered on top of the leaves
raging and dying. All this is

unknown to grackles; they live
without much raging and die
without much singing. They spit
up blood with hardly a word.

There is no last great vanity,
no final sobbing, no amorous
thumping, no double sadness
in peculiar fifths. If they do sing

it is an ascending squeak,
more like a rusty hinge,
more like a grating. There was
a crow I knew sang *Tosca*,

she plunged her beak into
her ravager's breast, she cawed
with happiness, she gurgled,
but that was different. This sky

will have no moon till five
in the evening, we will have to
contend in the morning. I will
fall from the parapet first

or she can crumple a leaf up
for one of her letters. In my version

I would have let the politics
sneak in much more, that is

the edge love needed. I would have
modernized it—something
from after the war, either Nixon
or Senator Joseph disguised

as a scorpion; J. Edgar Hoover
getting his files together,
getting ready for his blackmail
or in the other—that sweet other—

when Mimi dies I'd fall
under the hubcap, I'd sing
my last good song in the voice
I lost at thirteen, in the style

of Bobbie Breen; he was
a boyhood singer—all mothers
wept at his sound. I am
at this late date, December

1991, on a street corner
in Jersey City the poet
Rudolpho—I am a Rudolph—
and I am burying Mimi

who died by flying away
somewhere over a bakery
when boredom finally took her.
This is the truth though my music

makes light of it. I tore
a leaf for her and fasted
for fifteen minutes though nothing
was there. I felt some dread

but that gave way to sleepiness
and fluctuations of the mind,
mostly a dark red cardinal
that Puccini must have invented

for his own undoing, "alone"
in her redbud, "lost, abandoned,"
and—God—I hate to say it
but—only for me—a kind of

cross between a toucan
and a sparrow, doing his laments
at the top of his voice, his false one
to be sure, stabbing his wives

one by one—a specialty—
making his savage speeches,
writing his bitter letters
on his legal pads, a toucan

of anger, a sparrow of shame,
piling the words up, turning them
into poems, then dying
on *his* hill of leaves, a Rudolph

beyond all Rudolphs, Pagliacci
secundo, Siegfried der wanderer,
Tristan der melancholish, Alfredo
der ethical, der loyal, dear Mimi.

Hinglish

Sacre Dieu, I said for the very first time
in my adult life and leaned on a tuft of grass
in the neighborhood of one green daffodil
and one light violet, and one half-drooping bluebell.

I did a stomp around my willow, driving
the cold indoors and letting the first true heat
go through my skin and burn my frozen liver.

I placed the tip of my tongue against my teeth
and listened to a cardinal; I needed at least
one more month to stretch my neck and one
for delayed heartbeats and one for delayed sorrows.

"Speak French," she said, and dove
into the redbud. "Embrassez-moi," I said.
"Love me a little," "I am waiting for the hollyhock
and the summer lily," she said. "I am waiting
to match our reds. Baisez-moi," she said,
and raced for the alley. "Here is a lily, my darling,
oranger than your heart, with stripes to match
and darker inside than you." "Parle Français,
mon cher; pick me a rose; gather roses
while ye may; lorsque tu peux." "Have you
read Tristan Tsara?" I said. "Suivez-moi,
there is a bee," she said. "Forget your mother,
Oubliez vos fils vos mères." Her voice
is like a whistle; we used to say, "what cheer,"
and "birdy, birdy, birdy." There is a look
of fierceness to her. She flies into the redbud
without hesitation. It's easier that way. She settles,

the way a bird does on a branch; I think
they rock a little. "Nettles are nettles," she says,
"fate is full of them." "Speaka English," I say

and wait for summer,
a man nothing left of him but dust
beside his redbud
a bird nothing left of her but rage
waiting for her sunflower seed
at the glass feeder.

"A single tear," I say.
"My tear is the sky you see it," she says. She has
the last word. Halways. A bird is like that. She drops
into the hemlocks. Her nest is there. It is
a thicket at the side of the house. "I hate
the bluejay," she says. In Hinglish. She flies to the alley
and back to the street without much effort though my yard
is long as yards go now. How hot it will be
all summer. "Have you read Éluard?" she says.
"He avoided open spaces; his poems
were like my bushes and hedges; there in the middle
of all that green a splash of red; do you like
'splash of red'? His instrument was the wind.
So is someone's else." She has a flutelike
descending song; when she speaks French the sky
turns blue. "On sand and on sorrow," he said. "He talks
just like you. He had a small desert too;
he had an early regret. There is a piece
of willow. I am building something. I'll speak
Hinglish now. I love simplicity.

I hate rank." "Little wing of the morning," I say.
"In the warm isles of the heart," says she.
"I hold the tenderness of the night," say I.
"Too late for a kiss between the breasts," say she.

sitting on my porch,
counting uprights, including the ones on my left
beside the hammock, including the ones on my right
beside the hemlock,
reading Max Jacob,
speakin' a Hinglish.

Did I Say

This time of year I kneel on my jacket. The ice
is almost solid. The groaning has ended. There is
an inch of fresh snow. A bush has turned to glass.

I take my left glove off, finger by finger.
There is a pocket in which I wait. I break
a twig. I pull at the bark. I give myself

to the first flower, something streaked with pink
and three dark leaves as a kind of foil, something
just two or three inches tall. As soon as it melts

the snow will turn to water; I will scrape
the ground a little; I will clean it. I am
cloven; I was split in two; I opened

because of the water, because of the seed. I thought
the knowledge had started—for half a day. I thought
the light was in one place, the dark in another.

I reached my left hand out; I let it tremble.
I looked at the sun, it was a kind of dandelion,
though smaller, it was a snowdrop, one of the leaves

was shaped like a goat, we stood and butted, I was
one side, he was the other, I ate the horns,
I ate the flattened eyes; light will cover

darkness—in a day or two—the flower
will be a snowdrop—did I say that?—the petals,
they are like rays. I walked for an hour struggling

with this and that; the split is harder and harder every year. I wrenched my shoulder—did I say that too? Did I say I was winged and scattered?

Finding the Bush

There is no shame in this, I left one bush
for another, one was smoking, one the flowers
were dry and brown; I planted them in a hat
and put them beside my bed; one bush was mostly
wood, the flowers were red of course and the fruit,
if that was fruit, was hanging down. I had to
either kneel or bend half over to drink the spikes
and when I set fire to it it was almost
the end of winter, at least by the calendar,
though I knew we could both still freeze. The shadow,
it didn't have wings, it wasn't a voice, it didn't
live unconsumed, but I still listened and also I
watched. I can't say pity, I can't say fear
either; I was enchanted—can I say that,
and use that word without reproach?—I was
enamored, and I kept coming back. I put
my hand inside the leaves but I was burned
and cut, my blood mixed with the fire; I was
destroyed for a minute, some small bush, a thorn
without much body, a jujube of sorts, had caught me
and left me; and I walked back, as I always do,
with a flushed face, mostly anger, and a drop
of sadness in the eye. Regret took over
after a minute, self-accusations, and even
talking aloud to myself. Whatever city
I live in, whatever steps I have to climb,
and when I walk up a hillside, I am both
enslaved and freed. I have reached a point
where they are almost the same; it is a relief
knowing that. As it was a relief
finding the bush, though I was looking for

something larger, either a woody astringent
such as you bury your face in, such as the end
of winter when the thaw comes suddenly blooms
with yellow flowers; or a kind of palm
with heavy cornstalks for a trunk and sticky
gardenias for a blossom, not that jujube.

Blacker than Ever

You should know this, who live in your own decade,
I never darkened mine nor took excessive pity
on my own life even though it was as black
as one of yours, and loved its Käthe Kollwitz
and its Paula Modersohn-Becker with a dead tulip
in one hand and a piece of cracked porcelain in the other.

I didn't sleep through the fifties—nobody did;
I lived on a hall in New York City and ate
from two white plates; I listened to Ralph Vaughn Williams
and Mendelssohn's Fourth and all of Vivaldi; I traveled
three times, I think, from Hoboken to Antwerp
and read my Auden and read my Roethke and stood
on the corner of Twelfth and Market in Philadelphia
in 1956 and pleaded for Stevenson
and studied medieval Latin—you should
try that combination, or one of your own.

For the record I'll say that I was standing
inside the front door of the Tyler Art School
in 1961 when Ad Reinhardt walked through
to spread a little bitterness. He was wearing
a black beret, as I recall, and a black
T-shirt and a black gabardine suit coat.
I was in exile at Tyler for wearing corduroys
and for comparing Creon to Kennedy.
I was the one-man English department and railed
freely from my Beckett and Stein. I taught
the Downfall and I taught the Jubilation.
I loved the smell of turpentine above all
things; I ate with the models and helped one buy
a 1953 Studebaker. We kissed

behind the malachite gearshift and we ate
foot-long poisonous hoagies. I sleepwalked
in front of City Hall against the president
during the little war with Cuba and stared
in agony at my few humiliated friends
shuffling back and forth on the mayor's sidewalk.

As far as the W.P.A. I was too young
by ten years for the eighty-seven dollars a month,
but I was not too young to wander between
the two great schools of Union and Columbus,
nor was I too young to walk down Fourth Street buying
bags of books. My grandmother's husband Jacobson
died on his knees in Homestead climbing a hill
with herring and chicken in his arms; the arteries
were still in darkness then. My uncle Simon
lived—after his attack—for twenty-seven years;
he was so small, my uncle, he wore boy's
clothing. He was rich in the twenties, he drove
a Pierce-Arrow—I remember the headlights
rested on the fenders like breasts, but he was a
failure most of his life—and bitter. In the thirties,
the bitter thirties, he went from door to door
collecting dimes for Metropolitan Life
or sat in his living room reading Emerson. Late
in his life—in his sixties, I think—he worked as a salesman
for Robert Hall, in downtown Detroit. I think it
was Cadillac Square. He was vice-president
of the local. In his eighties we sat on a sofa
in Miami Beach looking at the scrapbook
of photos and clippings, he and Soapy Williams,
he and Humphrey—in Atlantic City—at the

annual meeting; he was the smallest of the small
at the head table, and smiling the hardest. He sat
beside me in Beth Raphael crying, because
we were strangers there, because he was dying,
because we were mayflies, because we burst from the water.

Reinhardt died in his studio, he dropped down
beside a wooden easel; he was painting
something blacker than black—I wish I knew
the history better. I was probably swimming
the day he died. If it was in the morning
I could have been on the way to the pond; if it was
late afternoon I could have been half-sleeping
either inside the cabin or in the grass
half-listening to a song. I grieve for his death
as if I just discovered it; he would be
seventy-nine if he were still living; on Christmas
he would be eighty. Christmas Eve. There is
a flattened spider in my book, between
the color plates and the chronology—there would be
of course; her legs are facing left; her body
is shaped like a bow tie; she is more brown than black,
maybe it is the blood. I'm sure she thought
Reinhardt was like a brother, I'm sure she thought
that I would love it, but Reinhardt is more like a bee
than a spider, more like a wasp. Imagine him
eating away at his own nest, just imagine
a huge broom, his soul like five hundred insects
fighting the broom. Reinhardt believed, I think,
in annihilation—he was ruthless—his blackness
was and was not a blackness; I know that
myself; but I have different rules; for example,

I do love color, I do love light, I have
a yearning for form, I love to *sketch*, that is,
I love the hand as well as the mind; and I can't
remain aloof, and I can't disappear, and I can't
absolve myself by draining my life of oil
the way he did; and I am opposed to monotony
and timelessness—and even detachment; at least
I am a little worried. I guess his purity
is what I resist. But we were heartless the same way,
and we were thorns, and we loved gloom and believed
in clarity. I wish we could sit and talk.

In 1967, the year he died,
I reversed my life; there had to be
some wandering there and if not I'll claim it
anyhow; I'll sit at my dining room table
invoking his touchy spirit. There is a quail
I use, a painted clay, with startled eyes,
and there is a fish named Ivan Carp who reads
my poems and criticizes them; he is
a fish beyond all fishes and he swims
passionately at my table, beside the quail,
a carved pine with cones glued on for scales,
made by a sculptor in Pennsylvania—he put
a touch of red in the tail—it actually *swims*;
and when it comes to my journey he knows it so well
I can consult with him on the turns I took
inside the muddy roots and through the grasses,
although he is loath to talk about the future
or give me much advice. "We are swimming," he says,
"into the ocean, be careful, the water is clean here,
you are exposed, you will starve." It is

a paltry allegory, he is crude
and simple, being made of wood. I think
Paula Modersohn was a carp and Reinhardt
was a kind of carp although for the one
the agony of her life slipped into the art,
or *was* the art; and for the other he hated
that kind of agony—"Art comes only from art,"
is what he said, "any meaning demeans
the beauty"; and above all else he hated
images. The place of *his* agony—
I think I could describe it if I had to,
if I were going to do it. For my own
the carp says, "Quiet, root in the mud, feed
yourself at the bottom, lie in the sun, swim,
just swim." For me it wasn't his blackness and it wasn't
hers; I had my own just sitting beside
my uncle or leading my students down the steps
of the gallery at Tyler. While I was singing,
while I was being heartless, I also was doing
something else, the thing I try to explain
as I am sitting in an armchair or standing
in front of a birch tree. I do it constantly,
and understand it—as I should. I'll say
at least this much: the quail, when she whistles,
and when she looks at the chandelier with one eye
and the red carp with the other, she understands
too. My uncle Simon, named for God knows what,
named for a high priest, named for a slave; poor Simon,
who carried a cross, who shone in the Beth Raphael,
he understood. It was his knowledge. Waking up,
drinking my tea, haranguing, that was mine.

Only Elegy

I couldn't change the image I had of her
for the one thirty years ago of her singing Piaf
and the one twenty years ago of her waiting
on a bench in Kennedy for her first trip to France,
nor could I change the image of her standing at the sink
or the one of her methodically ripping up newspapers
for the one of her drowning in blood and the one of her coughing
whenever air came into her closed-up windpipe,
the "Get Well Soon" balloon rising above
the blue lobelia and the pink fleabane,
balanced as it was on a dowel, supported as it was
under its plastic chin by some folded ribbon,
over the fluvium basins, one pink and one blue,
under the stanchion, beside the folded wheelchair
and the dirty sheets and the machine at the next bed pulsing,
the name on the door in brass, "Irving Flegelman,"
"In Loving Memory of Irving Flegelman,"
"In Tribute to Leo and Sarah Zack," "For William
Malumet," "For Mr. and Mrs. S. Fine,"
"For Israel Zaigwell," "For Joseph Goldberg," "For Hetty
Rosenthal," "For Miss Rose Gould," "In honor
of Harriet Corman," "In Honor of Natalie Wise,"
and "Dedicated to Mr. and Mrs. Bogen."
For Ida Barach, born in Poland, died
a little north of Miami, who with her husband
Harry lived and loved and was estranged
on the east coast of America. Now you can love her.

Ida

Well, I am like a palm tree,
the plant of pure ugliness,
somewhere in a front yard
spared by the last hurricane,
one of the royal ones
whose glory is turned to scum,
whose riches are turned to rubbish.
It is as if its skin
was chiseled, it is as if
its hair was ripped from its head,
its dirty squirreltail fronds
turning brown on the sidewalk.
It is as if the wind
was showing it some kind of love,
the light beams of Plotinus
straight from the stars, like arrows
pointing down, like eyeballs
pointed up, the arrows
of our desire more broken,
more curved, the music coming
in English as well as Italian,
Pavarotti singing "Wien, Wien,"
my mother on the edge of her bed
staring at the lighted box,
her throat not yet closed up,
her own eyes wet with song,
a fixed smile on her lips,
her longing for the past so keen
it breathed in her, the moon
now gone from her life, the light
on the bay now gone, the Florida

of anger and melancholy
also gone, Pavarotti,
a fat angel with a beard
dressed in a silk tuxedo
with a handkerchief in his hand
singing and singing, and she,
poor Ida, poor Ida, still sitting
and smiling; it is as if
there was a kindness, as if
there was a thought to her pain,
as if the scarves in her dresser
could save her, or even the letters,
as if the bird-of-paradise
I sent her was not a simulacrum,
its yellow crown vibrating
on a true head, its blue beak
thinking, as if it prayed
the way a bird does that's shaped
like a gaudy plant—"Oh palm tree,
look at me shaking my head,
look at the red and green
flash in, flash out, may your eyes
be open to our distress,
we have polluted your name,
we have acted corruptly,
Thou art truly just—"
made of threads, you know,
a kind of netting, the flesh
is more than flesh, I hate it
because it expands by cracking,
because it grows in segments

and bends half over, because
of the swelling in the middle,
because the dead leaves envelop
the trunk, because it is home
to a thousand insects, it is
a kind of forest, because
the old skin is like burlap,
because I can't breathe, because
we sweat in Florida, because
Pavarotti and his handkerchief
are drenched, because my mother
is moving her lips—you know
how it is, the small birds drop in
and out, they stab at each other,
an airplane is booming, an ambulance
is passing by; she was
afraid of dogs, what would she
do in this swamp? The fruitwood
she loved is swollen, the wormholes
were painted on, the sun
ruined every surface, the green rug
is stiff and pale, the metal
is rusty, the lampshades are gone.
She lived here twenty-seven years,
Ida of the plain song,
Ida of Sigmund Romberg,
Ida of the Strausses,
Ida and her Henry,
Ida and her Jimmy,
Ida and her Harry,
Ida standing at the rail

of *The Song of Norway*, her hat
about to blow off, or standing
in front of St. Marks, the pigeons
eating at her heart, or Ida
dressed like Lillian Russell
the last night out in a harbor
in Venezuela or watching
La Bohème at the Nixon
in downtown Pittsburgh and eating
afterwards at Buon Giovanni's
or reading *Anna Karenina*
on the back porch on Vine Street,
her father smiling, the blue-eyed
distant saint, St. Beryl
the chicken killer, the scholar,
my secret and sorrowful mother.

Small Sunflowers

For Kathleen Peirce

I never saw three disks like that
    facing in all directions.
It was enough to make me think three winds
    were all there were,
and I loved the leaves that fed them. I stayed with them
    through thick and thin,
until the seeds themselves turned black and died,
    until their necks were broken
and half their faces were rubber and half were cotton.
    But first the gold dust fell
and they who prayed like any others, no they
    who almost knelt down,
whose shoulders were always bent, they gave the blessing.
    And such it always was,
the poor give to the poor. But in this case
    I saw millionaires
showering in that gold, one kind and another,
    from generals to bishops;
or our kind, whatever it is, even the young,
    those very little ones
who never earned what they spent and therefore were ignorant
    of what the sorrow is
and what the greed could come to. They must have prayed
    for mercy, that comes to me first,
and after that for wisdom, such huge flowers
    must pray for wisdom, not
for money, not for a job, or a prize, and not for
    their own yellow dust, they hardly
knew their own, there were so many, they prayed
    for everyone's dust, not one of them

was rude, not one was greedy, none of them
    rolled his eyes, none of them moaned,
or rocked his body, although it is not bad
    to do it a little. I live
in water as they do and I have gone as they do
    from place to place, although
I don't get ruined as they so quickly, I am not
    dry and broken, my leaves
aren't curled and lifeless, my crown isn't bent half over,
    my face isn't green, my petals
don't hang in the wind and fall like uprooted hair
    nor do I float in filth, but I
am sickened by lying and I am at last disgusted
    by the same corruption as they are
and I am frightened by the same destruction.
    The friend who gave them to me,
she was leaving, she was uprooted, and this
    was a way for her to stay here
and leave a trail, or surprise me or give me
    something new to go with
the dead honeycomb beside my bed. I hope
    the peaches are good there. I hope
she won't be vexed as long as I was.

The Jew and the Rooster Are One

After fighting with his dead brothers and his dead sisters
he chose to paint the dead rooster of his youth,
thinking God wouldn't mind a rooster, would he?—or thinking
a rooster would look good in a green armchair
with flecks of blood on his breast and thighs, his wings
resting a little, their delicate bones exposed, a
few of the plumes in blue against the yellow
naked body, all of *those* feathers plucked
as if by a learned butcher, and yet the head
hanging down, the comb disgraced, the mouth
open as if for screaming, the right front chair leg,
seen from a certain angle, either a weapon
or a strong right arm, a screaming arm, the arm
of an agitator; and yet at the same time the chair
as debonair as any, the brown mahogany
polished, the carving nineteenth century, the velvet
green, an old velour, as if to match
the plumes a little, a blue with a green. No rabbi
was present, this he knew, and no dead butcher
had ever been there with his burnished knife
and his bucket of sand; this was the angry rooster
that strutted from one small house to another, that scratched
among the rhubarb, he is the one who stopped
as if he were thinking, he is upside down now
and plucked. It looks as if his eye can hardly
contain that much of sorrow, as if it wanted
to disappear, and it looks as if his legs
were almost helpless, and though his body was huge
compared to the armchair, it was only more
horrible that way, and though his wings were lifted
it wasn't for soaring, it was more for bedragglement

and degradation. Whatever else there was
of memory there had to be revenge there,
even revenge on himself, for he had to be
the rooster, though that was easy, he was the armchair
too, and he was the butcher, it was a way
to understand, there couldn't be another, he had to
paint like that, he had to scrape the skin
and put the blotches on, and though it was
grotesque to put a dead rooster in an armchair
his table could have been full, or he just liked
the arrangement, or he was good at painting a chair
and it was done first—although I doubt it—or someone
brought him the bird—a kind of gift—for food was
cheap then, and roosters were easy to cook; but it was
more than anything else a kind of Tartar,
a kind of Jew, he was painting, something
that moved from Asia to Europe, something furious,
ill and dreamy, something that stood in the mud
beside a large wooden building and stared at a cloud,
it was so deep in thought, and it had tears
in a way, there was no getting around that kind
of thinking even if he stood in the middle of the room
holding his paintbrush like a thumb at arm's length
closing one of his eyes he still was standing
in the mud shrieking, he still was dying for corn,
he still was golden underneath his feathers
with freckles of blood, for he was a ripped-open Jew,
and organs all on show, the gizzard, the liver,
for he was a bleeding Tartar, and he was a Frenchman
dying on the way to Paris and he was
tethered to a table, he was slaughtered.

Fleur

For Laraine Carmichael

No sense lying—my own two rows of pompoms
are still alive, even in November, the frost
of October twelfth meant nothing. Here I am
watching marigolds, in the dark. Can you
believe it? What do you think they looked like? Why
was I denied those little buttons, those small
orange clusters? These are like trees, and branch and divide,
they cover my daisies, they ruin my iris, there is
a forest here! How can I scoop the dirt up
with my own nails and rend my hair? There isn't
a single thing here for me to love, I feel
belittled. Where are the leaves? How can these flowers
live without leaves? It could have been the snapdragon
with swollen blossoms and dark spots in the throat,
it could have even been the daisy, Lord they
grow to supernatural heights, but there is
wisdom somewhere. I could have walked through daisies
sucking my cheeks. I could have lain like a swan
with eyelashes intact and pulled the *fleurs*—
they are called *fleurs*—she loved me all that morning,
she loved me not, she hates me, she despises me,
she was my lily, she is, or was, my lavender,
she was my delphinium, short and blue. I count
my *fleurs*, I have a way to go. I see me
walking the borders, my hands are in my pockets,
the railroad ties are *planks*, I turn to the left,
I am ready at any minute to plunge
into the marigolds and rub my hair
with maroon *fleurs*; or I am ready to cut
one or two branches and bring them inside. I have

a bucket of orange and yellow. I add some honey
and marjoram and bitters, I can rinse
my face when I want to, say all winter, and I can
start next time with *flats*, some Crown of Gold
for early rising, some Yellow Cupid for roaring,
and bury whatever is left out there, three stalks
with curled dried-up leaves, and heads bent down
like rubber mops and one small dragon, its throat
painted scarlet and three or four ox-eyed giants
with *fleurs* like impoverished nails, like filed teeth,
hanging on, I guess, to love, she loves me,
she loves my crumbling leaves, she loves my spikes,
she loves my broken stalks, she loves my mop,
and I love hers though mostly I love the light
that comes from her—her *emanation*—did I
ever think I'd say that?—and the coneflower
that rotted for two or three weeks—I loved that—
and how my fate was sealed by which direction
the stem would fall and whether the head would drop
before the leaves, and how she knew it, my *fleur*.

St. Mark's

Still like a child, isn't it?
Climbing up an iron staircase,
arguing with some Igor
over the broken lock,
letting my head hand into the sink,
rinsing my neck with cold water.

Like a wolf, wasn't it?
Or a dove that will never die.
Reading Propertius, trampling
the highest stars,
forcing my hands together,
touching the row of snow-capped garbage cans.

Swaybacked, wasn't it?
Dragging my wet feet
from one park to the other.
"Softened by time's consummate plash,"
isn't it?
Tulip of the pink forest.
Red and yellow swollen rainwashed tulip.

Two Things

I have balanced two things, the black-faced
cardinal and the black-eyed bluejay

and lived beside the red chopping block
two flights down. I have wandered

under the floorboards near the drifting
walls and I have seen the joists

forced into stone. I have loved
the same blue spark as Cicero loved

and put my chair under the lightbulb
where, for three hundred hours, the darkness

was displaced. It was that darkness
I read in—or on the fringe. I read

on one side of the line where the two
changed forces; there it was sudden; I

was in a kind of circle of light,
in a kind of *beam* that forced

the darkness away though where on my arbor-
vitae or where in my hemlocks the two

abounded I don't exactly know
unless the two birds I have balanced

have something to do with it. Wisdom
they found by flying and landing; happiness

by eating—and singing—though the shadows
divided them too, and when they strayed

too far into the light they were
exposed and flew back into the trees

for safety. I finished Cicero
and sat there like a flower, the dust

came through the knotholes, there was a kind
of wind, there was a gusting without

much of a difference in heat and cold,
nor were there layers though close to the walls

and close to the dirt underneath the floorboards
it was colder, as it was hotter

under the bulb itself where Cicero
shook a little in my hands,

not from the wind so much, and I
mourned his exile as I mourned

his hatred and I longed for justice
in Rome—imagine that!—I turned

the bulb with my hand, I used my scarf
so I could bear the heat, it was

yellow and brown, my third wife lost it
in less than an hour, I used to wear it

more like a shawl, I used to sing
to the arborvitae, I loved both birds;

I did without a bedroom, I did
without a dog. I lived for one thing

so there was one light, it was connected
by a single thread, there was one darkness

and it was connected too; the birds,
I was their windfall, I was their sorrow.

Knowledge

Take water and fire, any disturbance between them
would be disastrous; or take me and this baby buggy
sitting half protected and half exposed in the lindens
and under the lindens and on the farthermost side
of one of the lindens, light there almost filtering,
almost feathering down; or take the nurse there,
the book of Hofmannsthal in her hands, an orange
for later, four or five cold pierogi, her blue
sunglasses, all that she gathered up before she
left, and take the last three days of the war
and how she will spend her time with a photograph
and two ruined letters, rubbing her legs at night
with liniment, remembering how his left hand rested
under her head and how his free fingers touched
her hair—the flock of black goats—and that his lips
were like two lilies; and Austria gone and even
the mountains lost, her unity shattered, a torpor
taking over—an anguish—and how she heard about it
opening the window, there was a weary voice
under a hat, she picked a flower out of the
windowbox, she couldn't believe it, he would
rest here, there would be no mud, she would guard
his breath, every two hours she would listen
and touch him on the forehead; her cheeks, she supposed,
were like two halves of a peach, her eyes were a little
red, they needed touching; the veterans would grow
more and more bitter, they would even burn the
old stone buildings, she supposed; her neck was
made of ivory, she supposed, her belly
was a heap of wheat—he said that over and over—
a heap of wheat encircled with lilies; her knowledge

came from death and defeat; she walked from one
fire to the next; they stood there in the cold
with only brooms, chewing on God knows what,
dazed with knowledge, their feet swollen, their eyes
swimming in milk, thinking of living again.

Sixteen Minutes

There in the sky above Lewisburg
were two land masses that looked so much like clouds
that when two birds flew through them
they flew through livid chimneys and smoking hillsides.

One was Ireland and one was Long Island,
side by side at last,
completely forgetful of the other two masses,
one to the east of those islands, one to the west.

I parked my car, as I do, at a deadly corner
to watch them change or come together as one more
land mass or even to join the other continents
they left behind in Wal-Mart's cloudy parking.

I noted everything
including the great salt ponds in eastern Long Island,
including the dark blood all over Ireland,
caused, as it were, by the sun.

Wild ducks flew over one place
and wild geese over the other;
crows, with strips of something hanging from their mouths,
flew between them.

I tried, without going to the library,
to unravel the history. Especially
I thought of illegal landings and I thought
of the little white potato passing between them.

Strange to think that they had different poets,
so close they were together, and strange to think

how it would be if ours were closer or theirs
were closer to us or if they drifted together

east of New York and west of England or in
the lower sky above this Lewisburg east
of Clarion, Pennsylvania, west of Bloomsburg,
three hours from Philadelphia, five from Pittsburgh.

Odd to think of the Jews and Irish too,
how we married each other,
how my own children have pink faces,
how we hated each other, Jews and Irish,

and fought each other, how the Jews were horrified
by one thing, how the Irish were enraged
by another, how the Irgun on our side
and the I.R.A. on theirs both battled English

smugness and deceit, how they both saw through it,
and how the English were appalled by them both,
not to mention the Irish down from Canada
who settled in Queens, not to mention the mayor

of Dublin himself a Jew whom I saw plant
a tree in the old Sephardic graveyard on Arch Street
in Philadelphia I am sure who traveled
from Jewish place to Jewish place and planted

and talked and drank and told a joke albeit
wearing a top hat not a derby and not a
cap—the thing we had in common—certainly
not a beret and not a yarmulke, the wind

our enemy, destroying a couple of counties
in both good places, me not wanting to see
the world in shreds. Language too we had
together, I would call it subversive, and spoke we

still another tongue and spoke we this tongue
as gorgeous strangers; and theater, I would name
theater, and comedians and actors and lightweight boxers
and singers, by the dozen, and music of tears

you might call soft from time to time and blarney,
a Jewish characteristic, mostly though
self-reproach—we couldn't help it—one cloud
turned black, and then the other, they were raking

their own furnaces; there was a little
crime too, and there was the mother, we both
sang "Mammy," how could we help it?—Mammy, Mammy,
I'd walk a million miles for one of your towels

Oh Mammy; but God we were different. Did I say
how one cloud was different from the other and how
I sat there for sixteen minutes till one island
then the other fell apart? Truth was

they fell apart slowly, truth was a larger
island came in view, I guess it was Greenland
or part of Alaska had mingled with Siberia
and carried it my way; I almost made a new

religion in those sixteen minutes and a new
language, Judish, and a foggy city

called Irishaloyem—that would mean
Peace to the Irish. I say peace to the Irish

and I say peace to the Jews, and I say—grudgingly—
peace to Greenland and peace to the monster Siberia
with Alaska in its mouth and peace to
the hills of Pennsylvania and mostly peace

to the inmates of Lewisburg Penitentiary
and to the Irishman there we held illegally
and Thornburgh extradited as a last vicious act
to make Bush smile and Queen Elizabeth chuckle,

and Jimmy Hoffa and the Berrigan brothers
and Greenglass the rat who checked his atom bomb in
before they gave him a number and Morton Sobel
who spent twenty years here because he kept his bomb

in a cardboard suitcase underneath a girder
on the Williamsburg Bridge; and good Alger Hiss, he came here
for the air and for the food, he had
a cardboard suitcase too with a bomb inside it;

and peace to that Irish Jew, Wilhelm Reich,
who died inside his cage in 1957
and to the love he brought us and to his exploding
cells and to the cloud that carried him up;

and to the shawls we wore and to our moaning
and to the stone walls we moaned against and the moon
we always kept track of, the moon that ruled our lives
through all the killing and hounding, we all but worshipped.

Picking Asters

Now he knew the sycamore was imitating
him, holding its one leg under a rock,
bending to wash its face. He no longer fought
the mottled trunk or smashed his hollow stick
against its thighs; even when he hung
his steaming washrags on a lateral branch—
a left arm in the air—he did it gently,
almost as if to warm those muscles. Life
was precious to them both now, one hanging
over a river, one in a slatted chair;
one at his tea, one at God knows what kind
of muddy beer. He saw it coming, he was
ready for it, and he could have sat for hours
just staring, but he was starting to imitate
the tree—a sycamore—he threw himself
into his stretches, he screamed at the river. High up,
maybe on the road, it might seem funny,
the man stretching and shouting, the tree still
and bent, but on his face already there were
signs of pain. The act of him picking asters,
the act of him keeping his right hand out to keep
his balance as he bowed—if the tree itself
were not bowing like that, if there weren't asters
planted in its nether paw, you'd say
he had to be foolish, if he weren't barking, if he weren't
trying to catch his breath you'd say he was dancing.

Most of My Life

A squirrel eating her way in and a mother cardinal
with such an eye she knew two things at once
in what was work for her lower than me here
I'm sure as close to her nest as she would allow
without engaging her whole prudent being, and I
saying cheer to her, what cheer, what cheer,
breathing my own prudent last if that was necessary,
my heart going out to her, for all she knew
my feet like bird's feet—I could be her child,
if it were necessary, and die on a thorn
or wear a dress for her and sparkle as rain does
and wear my sparkling beads and wear a sparkling
tear on my cheek or I could be as still
as she wants, I could be a stone, till her eye
is satisfied, she is so rough in these things,
she is so sloppy, look at her straw, she is
so close to my mother—is that Ida, her eye
shrewd and watching? Daughter of lilac, wife
of honeysuckle and privet—ah she has worked
and her heart is beating, she is a nurse, and a scholar,
and an architect, her slur and her rocking body
proof positive; she lands on my impatiens,
she flies to my birch, and I lie dead in her lap
and dead in the bark and dead in the grass stems, my arms
hanging out of the nest, leaves on my chest,
weeds and rootlets here and there, my stomach
a little red already and a little brown,
a twig in my mouth, but only by accident,
for there is more love than not, and she is reaching
to get the twig and I am holding on,

which is enough for one day, pity alone
enough for the two of us though there was grief
and duty too. I would have held up a lily
for her for she is not to blame; I would have
dried her tears. I did it for most of my life.

Essay on Rime

God knows those apes my father's relatives
born in the Ukraine and raised on white cheese and herring
will live till their hundred and twenties so I will be
careful when I tell my Ukrainian tales
and check all the cities from Novgorod to Dallas.

God knows, God knows, they lived on a small farm
owned by ethnic Germans and cut trees down
and studied for only a month a year in the autumn
and one in the spring. God the trumpeter knows
that one of them owned a stogie factory in Pittsburgh

and one was a dentist in Michigan and one
had a perfume shop on the rue Madeleine and drove
a Buick. Because of his luck and where he was sent
to sojourn during the first days of the War
one of them ended up in Florida filling

prescriptions and later cashing checks. I
who have the brains in the family, I ended up
on a wooden porch arguing with a swallow
and wrestling with a bluebell. My plan is now
to live in three places, maybe divide my books

and maybe divide my time. One of my houses
will have to be near Turkey since that is the way
to get back to the Crimea and the Sea of
Azov; and I have chosen Samos only
because Pythagoras rebuked the petty tyrant

Polycrates there by the waters of Ambelos;
and I could have a cat who eats his catch
behind the wet rocks and shakes his rear leg, and read
my American subscriptions and rant as I did
when I was twenty, even if I was alone, though

I would be, I think, surrounded as always
and listen to the sound of waves assembling
and count the intervals. Even the druggist,
even the parfumist, would understand that,
wouldn't they, my rich cousins who burned, the one

at Nice, the other at Coral Gables. I who
sat and slept for hours and knew the white crests
and the brown valleys and what they meant, and I
who loved the sun just as they did and burned
from the same fire I sang with my broken fingers.

Oracle

I have a blue chair; there is a blue rock
and a weed in flower just before the hill
begins in earnest. There is a little chorus
somewhere down there and something that lost its voice
a half a century ago is starting up
again; it was a tenor, it was a boy
soprano, it lives by itself, it is
disincarnate, it moves from C to C,
and it is in a valley beside some mint,
against a cherry. I sang my heart out. I learned
to pipe early, I held my arms out, I buried
one hand in another—so we could have something
to do with our wrists, so we could expand our lungs
at the same time, so we could warble, so we could last
forever. Consider the basso profundo that sang
as if he were a string, his voice expanded
and shook, consider the alto. The hair on my face,
the hormones in my heart, the flesh in my hand—
this is how a soprano just disappeared
and a hoarse baritone with a narrow range
suddenly took her place. The sun in the desert
going quickly down, the dark from nowhere, voices
droning, voices shrieking, I am grateful.

II.

Hot Dog

I.

One white mushroom lying in the street across
from Sappora East and one wicker baby carriage
with dogs inside and one New York telephone
with its mouth ripped off to go with my Augustine
and one mini tulip and one black girl named Hot Dog
sticking pins in her friends on Avenue A
to go with my Whitman and one of her friends skating
off the curb, Whitman and Augustine—
well, never seeing each other, though Whitman came later
and he saw Augustine and maybe Whitman
wandered through Carthage; he would have been a goat
and Augustine would have petted his bony head
and stared into his eyes. I hate to do this
but I am choosing one—you have to do it
one way or another, you can't smile walking
past the Japanese fruit store, you can't be
benign forever—fuck that!—one is an enemy
and one is a friend. C'est ca! I hate quitting
the world; the "marvelous light" they hunted for
is on my street, or should be; Hot Dog will know it
when she sees it. I'll be across from the square
at the Odessa Cafe arguing with the owner,
a greedy unshaven bastard who owns the laundromat
also and probably called the police to have
Hot Dog arrested, just for sticking pins—
not needles, mind you—into her friends—and enemies;
it was the one thing she did. They handcuffed her
and she was sitting on the curb; there were
five police cars and a righteous civilian
explaining it to the spokesman for the homeless

at Seventh and Avenue A; he was wearing
roller blades; he told me about the freedom
it gave him, how he almost felt released—
that was his word—how a pair of blades
was cheaper than a pair of shoes. I won't
engage the spokesman *or* the official, one
is arguing for depravity, he says Adam
was born corrupt, he says our only hope
was to admit our guilt, he says Hot Dog
will burn forever; the other defends children
who die in infancy, he says humans
have only themselves to blame, he says the species
will not be resurrected; what I say is
I should have married seven times, I should have
had two dozen children, I should have raised them
as Jews—or humanists—I should have lived
in France where I wanted, I should have bought nine houses—
three is not enough, I shouldn't have been
kind to my enemies, I should have left home
when I was sixteen—that was the time.

II.

                                                  I steal
a flower for Hot Dog, she would rather have
a dollar; there are blossoms on the street
and seeds and rubbish; if the gulls of Assateague
were here they would clean up, I don't see gulls
in New York City, not where I go. I plan
on shedding some blossoms this summer; I will walk
my half a day stopping only to study marsh crabs

on Avenue B and northern lobsters on Sixth.
I will follow a woman in a baseball cap
as long as I can; it is her thighs I love—
and her glasses. I will pretend she is a moon shell
and I am looking at the spots. Could I
maybe get away with it? I'll walk
to the German Library for a late afternoon
of study—at the chestnut table. "What is
regeneration in a starfish? Is there
rebirth as we know it in Helvétius
and Rev Akiba? Is it immortality?
Is there a mind in the stump? Is the starfish
a model for the Mexican sun? How scarlet
is it at the center?" The library closes
at seven o'clock. I usually fight all night
with whelks and get exhausted. I turn pink
from too much sand. A rose from Chincoteague
lies between two bivalves. I can remember
bending down to smell it; I hate roses
that have no odor. I close my eyes. Their teeth
are in their skulls; they are eating soup, and smoking;
a candle is on their table. I sit down
at another table—I am a step above them—
and eat my soup. My book is open to the page
on mushrooms; it is all right to eat them; nothing
suffers, there is no blood, there are no jaws
for grinding food, there are no organs; I rub
one of my eyes; seaweed would be all right;
kelp is all right; onions, potatoes, hollyhocks—
but only after they wither—magnolias, even
grass, though that is degrading for us, sea lettuce,

tulips. I have thirty-nine eyes, some of them
are only for light, but most of them are for vision
and I have been lucky. I am relearning some Law
and trying to find the connection; I had a friend
who drove all day to find the kosher buns
to go with her meat; she ate dinner with us
on Sunday afternoon, my Pennsylvania wife,
my Pennsylvania children; the Law was never enough
for her—more Law! more Law!—we could talk about it,
me with my lettuce, she with her buns; I am
a child still of my grandfather, sprinkling salt
on the open wounds, only he lived in a cage
and I lived in a field of clover and daisies.
I lay down there; we will talk about it,
fat that covers the inner organs, flesh
torn from a living creature, poor animals
killed by other animals, those that died
of internal causes, always the kid and the milk,
and always drinking blood and eating fish
that had no scales.

III.

                                    One of my father's brothers
believed in regeneration; he was careful
with each of his legs, he loved his fingers—holy,
holy, he said, ten times a day, holy;
holy, holy, he said it eleven times,
he touched his forehead, he touched his wrists. A chicken
had to be perfect, not one blemish. Disgusting,
blood between the toes, disgusting the neck

that's thinner at the base where skin hangs loose
as in a man with cancer. What I loved
was arguing with a Lutheran over the Law
and watching him suffer; over three coffee cups
a couple I knew reached out, they may have been Quakers
or radical Catholics, they were loving, they stood for
reason, above all else; we talked for an hour
about the forbidden—milk and meat—Maimonides
was at their side, he was their coach; they argued
hygiene and nourishment and toxic qualities
while I was for obedience to the Book,
for its own sake, and slavery to the words,
that is if you do it, truth is I didn't do it,
though truth is for years I suffered whenever I ate
pork—not bacon but pork—I thought it was sauerkraut
that made me sick, for years I thought that, you keep
kosher to show your love for the void, to make
a separation, to be one of the lambs—
although you do it out of pressure and fear
as well, and arrogance of the spirit—I think
it's called inflation, I have it a little myself,
not eating fat, no meat, no ice cream; I walk
around humming, I sneer a little, though how
could you slice a piece of meat from a living animal
or tear a limb off or eat from a broken neck
or something lying there dead? What are we, crows?
Are we leeches? How can we kill cows
and murder salmon? I the bore am asking it
who used to suck the marrow, who used to pick
the bones so clean there wasn't a speck of meat
left, or gristle—the bones were white; I even

chewed and swallowed them if I could; my wife
screamed at me—the lover of pork. Hog Dog
was back in two hours; when I gave her the dollar
she put it in her hair, there wasn't a pocket,
I think, although there were two skirts and a pair
of blue jeans under the skirts—it was her modesty
that kept her from hoisting them up and putting the money
in one of those pockets. Blue jeans have seven pockets
sometimes; somebody west of the Mississippi
stamped the rivets on, or a machine
did it, a western machine with a large white hat
for keeping the sun off and a pair of boots
for walking through the brambles and for rubbing
against a spotted side.

IV.

Augustine

fought one battle—although he fought many—we all
fight one battle, one a life—I think
that's mostly right. Whitman fought one. For which
he is denounced. Sometimes. I'm amazed
at my own battle; it's the same as it was
when I was twenty, the same mountains, the same
exhausted woods, the same city; Smetana
had one sound in his ear; I know three people
that have the ringing, the notes are always the same,
one or two loud notes, two of the three
are more or less sane; I walk between my avenues
singing my note; there is a dead bird lying
with his feet in the air and crosses for his eyes;

that is, his eyes are crossed, the eyes have truly
turned to x's. I remember the smell
of dead birds when I lived in Pittsburgh, there was
a certain rottenness, a sweetness, I would know
somehow long in advance the smell was coming,
and I would see it there, the broken wing,
blood on the neck, a beak gone, or a leg gone;
it was for me my loss. I would count
the steps—the yards—until the stench was bearable,
until it disappeared. There are two birds,
both dead, one has the belly and chest all eaten
so when I turn it over the fumes rise
from deep inside the feathers, she it is
who stopped for a roll I think from the Jewish bakery
on First Avenue, south of St. Mark's, the west
side of the street, I know by the twist; she left
most of it uneaten. I love how she waited,
how she thought, before she plunged her beak
into the roll. Now it's stale, the moisture is gone
and it will soon be covered with dirt. I counted
three dead bodies, not counting insects, between
First Avenue and Tompkins Square, the third
was a cat, that was the justice, one red cat
for every two birds, there is a scale, a thumb
is fixing the weight a little. His face was smashed
and one of the eyes was gone. The ants were there
cleaning it up—part of the justice; there were
rows of them, of course, but at the wellhead
they gave up the rules and rushed around the lid
eating and working. I have a thought—does his cry,
his soft mewing, have any weight? Is it

substantial, as they used to say? Does the song
of the bird have substance for that matter; can a row
of ants or, say, two hundred beetles lift it
and carry it into their holes? Can the song be eaten
and the notes be changed? Will they be ruined? Corruption
obsessed me there, the smell of that flesh, the sight
of broken and eaten bodies, our own nervousness
turned to garbage. It was the good diminished
of Augustine. I thought of him. Corruption
between my avenues. I thought of his battle
in front of my Moroccan restaurant or eating
my own roll; like him I entered into
my small body, as he would say; I saw
beyond my mind, as he would say, the light
he loved to write about, though I would mention
the streak over Tompkins Square above the playground
and what was unchangeable behind the seesaw
and how the darkness entered. I love that
as much as I do the other, that one moment
when light is lost a little, though it seemed
like some other force, a mauve or a purple.

V.

                                        I stared
at a carcass, as we all do, I had a thumb
inside my mouth against the bottom teeth
or I was holding my fingers against my temple
or I was pressing my palm against my forehead
or sometimes, as I do, I was half-scratching
the top of my head, though that could have been the sun,

it had to be in the nineties; I compared
the word "corpse" to the word "carcass"; I was
dying for a dictionary; I was
obsessing on death—the good smell helped me just there
west of the square, the good sun helped, it was
a compost pile, I myself was a beetle
of just that sort and crawled from heap to heap
pincing and chewing. In my case thinking. Whitman
was drifting from layer to layer. He would be
a fly. This time a fly. He thought of himself
as a midwife. "Accoucher," he said. He
and Socrates. He was astounded, flying
from stoop to stoop, from door to door, like that vile
first servant of God looking for blood, murderer
for whom I ask forgiveness. Whitman lay there
among the leavings, holding his breath. I mention
the stink of a refrigerator, the mixture
of coffee grounds and ruined T-shirts, but Whitman
called it the resurrection of the wheat.
He was able through his chemistry
to rescue the corpses, he could concentrate
on conversion, how the foul liquid and meat
turned into melons and apricots and roses,
none of which was poisonous—though death itself
was poisonous, he was too brave there, he just whistled
too much, he swaggered, north on First, as far
as I know, past Sappora East, though sometimes
he didn't swagger—I have to say that—death then
was truer, I'll call it truer, he even called it
exhilarating—it was his subject—sweet flag
rising out of his breast, a plump bird

singing dirges, a coffin half-floating past
the gunnysacks of rice, voices moaning
in Spanish and Korean, Yiddish driven
into a corner onto some seats in back of
a tiny theater on Second Avenue; I climbed
the stage, we would have turned it into the language
of feeling—we already did—we would have added
more complexity and more profundity
and borrowed less from the Russian and the English—
and voices moaning in Polish and Ukrainian
as one more coffin floated by: Forgive me,
Jew, Jew; forgive me, kike; forgive me,
you fucking turd; ah, where should we put the bell
now that the goat his throat is slit? Ah Jew,
fucking Jew.

VI.

                Christ, a watering can, I
didn't see it lying underneath the
rocking chair, there where the cane is split,
a green plastic with most of the handle gone,
the water of death now in it, foul rainwater
breeding mosquitoes, rain and a little food
across from the health food bakery. It was the
water of life I was confusing it with
and I would have held the can against my body
if there was a lily there or some small fleabane
growing through a crack, and soaked the crack
and everything around it. You could call
the water *breath* if you wanted, you could say

the water was breath, you could water the fleabane
by breathing on it. I expanded my lungs
across from the health food bakery; I walked
one way hard and one way easy because of
the wind; I was both shaking as I went
and shaking when I came back, the wind was in me
and it was on me, there were gusts, the *Times*
was everywhere, tree branches, such as they were,
were in the streets and garbage cans with numbers
out of sync were rolling down the sidewalk
and banging against the steps and rails; there even
was the sound of broken glass a house or
so away, maybe it was the deli where
dope was sold, maybe it was the door
above the jacked-up Lincoln, a fine rust job
with most of its own glass gone, a curved space
for a rear window, a shattered spiderweb
for a front window, no need to put the cardboard
in the side rear begging for mercy, pleading
the lack of stereo, the lack of almost anything,
everything already gone, and no need certainly
to lock the steering column with a club,
one of the signs of wrath; or maybe it was
only a cup that someone dropped from the sixth
or seventh out of hopelessness, the breath
almost gone, the effort making him gasp
and hold his pulse—or hers—or some flat green
depression plate that she—or he—had treasured
out of stupidity and pumped-up value
now that deflation was in the air and oxygen
was at a premium. I was slightly *fou*,

though I hate to put it that way, I get frenzied,
especially in the morning, the sprinkler has already
been there and the brushes have scarred the cement,
though who am I to be a bird at that hour
or some kind of walking plant, a six-foot daisy,
a truly great delphinium? I am a little
embarrassed; I would like not always to have to
be the one who sings, the one who does it
for others since they stand there dumb and dazed
or smiling like cuckoos. I would just as soon
breathe quietly at my kitchen table or at a
twenty-four-hour cafe or even in a
bed with roses over me and sunlight
starting to come through the slats, a little music
coming through the door. Ridiculous panting.
Ridiculous even talking. For years I lived
in expectation, that is the way I put it,
though that was the way a prophet put it—he
was living in expectation, though he meant
final days. I never thought it through,
I didn't think like that, I may have snorted
and felt a rush inside, I know I got dizzy
just standing, I know I had to walk to slow down,
and when I was forty I held on to a wall
to keep myself from falling—but I meant
that I would let the wind pass through me, that I
would feel my pulses pounding a little, not
that I would see the Republic revived or see
streets with dimes piled up or cigars pouring
out of bedroom windows the way they did
on Pine Street in Philadelphia when I dumped

a box of stale smokes onto the stoop
and the three men who were sitting there went wild
with all those riches. Neither did I mean
a spook would walk through the wall, like this, like this,
and rub the holes in his wrists and ankles and whisper
his nine last words, or his last thirty-seven—
We could talk about it. Breath fills the body,
there is no doubt about it, breath is the life
that made the bones to rattle, that is it made them
go wet with life—it was a blowing—and breath,
though it was called by another name, is what
condemned this world, it had that power, it was
the fire too, it lived in the heart, it was
a kind of person—at least a mouth—and shook
the doors; it was a broom, if anything
a broom, it set a bat at liberty,
it gave him sight, it was a forgiveness, he
was born this time of water, and blood, he bathed
in all the bristles, he was changed. And I,
who didn't shower at Auschwitz—you should forgive me
for mentioning it again—I breathed my fire
wherever I went; I guess of the two I was
the dragon, not the piddling Siegfried, I guess
you have to make a choice; I was the fog,
I knew the song of birds. Sometimes I stretch
to open my lungs; I practice storage, I close
and open my mouth, I force the air through the filters,
I sneeze, I close one nostril. I was able
when I was twenty to stay underwater for three
whole minutes—under a dock; it would have been longer
except they pulled me up. I found a way

to exhale a little, and float—in the dark—the light
was above me, and behind me; they were angry
and frightened that I stayed so long, and I
was sad I had to come up; I think only half
my air was gone, but who would believe that? I know
I held one hand to the moss and I know the weight
was gone from my body. Where was my wheezing? Where
was my heavy sighing? I swing my lateral arm,
I stretch my ribs, I tap my chest. Houdini,
as I recall, could not undo the straitjacket
or maybe it was the chain; he lost his will,
he couldn't control his air, he wasn't a flower,
the water couldn't keep him alive, though he was a lily
and that's why he died; his blood turned blue and his lung
turned to cardboard, poor magi—before he broke
his thoughtful head through the ice.

VII.

                                    When I was twenty
I held my hand against a wall and I had
trouble breathing when I was forty. I tried
a paper bag but I would always cut
the slits for my eyes too low and end up breathing
through one of my eyeballs. I began my studies
when I was four; I stood in line to eat
a cube of sugar. When I was five I was
a Christ-killer—what did I know? I killed Him
every Friday, every Sunday; I ate Him
on Saturday afternoon—with carrots, sweet
beloved brother Jeshua. I came home

bruised a little, some blood in my ear, a childish
tooth displaced. I read my Aesop Fables
when I was seven and when I was eight I learned
to love the locust; there was a woods across
the street from my house, but when I came back at thirty
the woods was gone and I was followed by a cop
who thought I looked suspicious; I was followed
once because I stood in front of a mansion
sketching in the vaulted windows, anger
pushed me into sketching, it always started
with something ruined; it took me a lifetime to learn
a little respect, I was an unknown follower
of Krishnamurti, and Robespierre, I thought
of one revolt or another, I was protesting
indecency, my specialty was cutting
through pounds of fat. I have a few good stories—
twenty, thirty—it's hard to believe them now,
now that I'm one of the olders. I am dying
to talk, my mouth is full of goodness, I
have turned it into romance, even to
myself but at the time I was a type of
worrier, a species of Amos. I
couldn't do it now but I attacked the governor
of Pennsylvania—he was a prick—and three
college presidents, they were harps without strings,
and lesser—and greater—fry. I am too happy
about it now, I should be in a cave
at this age, I should have some sorrow, I was
Diogenes for a while—I was his grandson
and carried a flashlight, maybe it was a little
Amos and a little Diogenes. Amos

should be on a stamp, the stamp would show him cursing
Harry Truman, or Ronald Reagan, maybe
LBJ, our dear cutthroat, or Bush,
who never got caught, or rat-faced Nixon, Nixon
the rat supreme, though Amos would love to harry
maybe a Kissinger, maybe a slightly less
lesser rat, but only slightly, maybe
one small stamp with shame in the corner, the word
"shame" in pink, the letters shimmering,
wavering, to call attention, but who
would sign for that? For someone doing the signing
would have no snout, not he, not she! His eyes
would never be bulging, he'd never not half rise up
and sniff the air, he'd never live in the sewers
and have a leather tail and grind his teeth
and leave a deadly smell, not he, not she!
He'd never not squeak—that was Stalin who squeaked!
That was Nero! I am getting ready
for my gold watch, I'd love to have one, I can
have a small pile of gold and not be ruined,
though when I was thirty, though when I was twenty-eight,
I had to turn it down. I turned it down
in Carl's Chop House, in Detroit, in old
Tambellini's, in downtown Pittsburgh, we were
sitting like smalltime lawyers and smalltime dentists
with handkerchiefs in our pockets. I was guilty
of worrying. How could I explain myself?
I had to leave. But I can keep the gold.
I have passed through. Like this! Ah, what would Tolstoy
say? He hated money. And he who lived on
air, the sixty-pounder with the loincloth
and wire glasses and crooked stick. I still

believe as I did, I never had a sudden
change, there wasn't a garden where a voice said
change, there wasn't a village where I lingered
and envied them and one day took off my shoes
and sang tra, la, la, la; when I did change
I turned a little little to the left
and to the right, I *focused* and I *simplified*,
something like that, I fused what I knew with what
I almost knew though when I look into
that third-story window I was *fou* all right,
and one day it is true I was pulling my hair
and flattening my head against the plaster
and trying to sleep, and waking up, then one day
I was benign. Was I a Buddha? I was
busy working, I was a dwarf. I scribbled
line after line, like this, like this, on any
envelope that came my way. I loved
in particular brown paper bags and either
cloth or paper napkins. Once I even
used a kind of tissue, you have to be
careful there, the paper sucks up the ink
and you have nothing left. I was forty-one
when all this happened, there was a crisis all right
but I did love the darkness of those two decades
and I still love that darkness as much as I love
the brightness, *hélas*, that followed. I didn't ruin
my life, I didn't for a minute ruin it. I
squandered my time—I still do that—but that is
savoring it. When I was twenty-seven
I found a pink hollyhock taller than I was
and I would have climbed up the green sides if only
I had wings, and I would have sucked the juices

and chewed the leaves. I was a principal
when I was twenty-six—I have the yearbook—
it shows me playing the harp, it shows me blowing
a rusty whistle. When I was thirteen I left
shul Yom Kippur afternoon and sneaked
back to my house; I ate a Bartlett pear
and I was free a little, but my stomach
was almost burning from my fear. I threw
the core into the toilet, my mother and father
never found out. That night at supper we ate,
I remember, some fruit and cheese but they
were irritable from fasting and from standing
half the day. That pear, I know, always helped me.
It made me stubborn. It gave me a certain detachment.
It kept me hidden. I can be in the middle of
anything because of that pear. When I was
shot in the neck in Newark, when I felt
the deadweight in my chest, can I not say
it was truly the pear? Why not! I'll say it! I
love being able to say it. I am confessing,
so I can say it. But I was insolent
for more reasons than one, and I was sarcastic
maybe to straddle some bitterness. Just today
I wanted to kill a black squirrel for breaking
the head of a daisy, a marguerite, he snapped
it off, I think he was crazy, no squirrel in this world
eats daisies. There in my beds of lavender
and lilies and bee balm and poppy I wanted to kill
him, maybe snap his head off, that crazy
black omnivorous squirrel.

VIII.

I followed Whitman
through half of Camden, across on the ferry and back
to Water Street; I lay down on his bed
and pushed my hand against the wall to bring
the forces back into my arms; I sang
something from *Carmen*, something from *La Bohème*,
and held my right hand up in the old salute
as music from my favorite regiment
came through the window glass as if to translate
not only the dust of those marching feet but the pails
of lopped-off arms and legs. I lay there thinking,
when I was dead—when he was dead—there would be
ten or more diseases, God knows what
they'd find if they cut him open, consumption, pneumonia,
fatty liver, gallstones, spongy abscesses,
collapsed lungs, tuberculosis of the stomach,
swollen brains. I lay there thinking his death
was lovely, just what he wanted. Mickle Street
was filled with people, for half a day, they stood
in front of the house and walked inside to stare
at the corpse. Thousands followed him to the grave
and filled up the giant tent or crowded the grass
around the tent, the grass he loved, the handkerchief,
the uncut powdered hair. How cunning it was
for them to walk on his head, he with that haircut,
he with that lotion, he whose grass kept growing
through all the speeches. Ingersoll was there—
he knew he would be—but he couldn't speak like the others
on the little bird going up and up; some Williams
you do not know read from Isaiah and Jesus

and later from Confucious and Gautama and Plato,
and someone spoke on the teaching and someone other
spoke on the immortality. Whitman lay there,
as far as I know, thinking about his house
and the ugly church across the street and the trains
banging and screeching a block away and all that
coal smoke and soot and the sweet odor that blew
across the river from the huge house of shit
on the Philadelphia side, but that was anyhow
the thing he loved, that shit, *n'est-ce pas?*—or he thought
of the day he spent with Burroughs walking in the sand
and smelling the ocean, how it was empty, it was
September already, the end of September, there was
much and copious talk, Whitman himself
was like the sea, he himself saw this lying
in the sand, his talk was sealike, Burroughs
himself saw it, Whitman thought the sea
was something beyond all operas—a little excessive;
he loved the surf the most, the hiss in southern
New Jersey sixty miles from Camden—he *was*
the sea, he knew that, though they dropped the dirt
now, they passed the shovel, someone threw
some pebbles, someone threw a flower, that was
the last time he would wander, what was the last
good thought? I ask this myself in Whitman's bed
after four hours of driving, after staring
out at his yard, he struggles with this, maybe
the hissing behind his poems, he likes that, he smiles—
a crumbling, sort of—maybe adhesiveness
again, he favored that word, or maybe
the world of matter, that would be good now, or how
he loved loose fish or how he hated that Concord—

was that uplifting enough?—maybe his room
on Mickle Street, the pile of papers, maybe
Oscar Wilde's visit, a dear young man, though Swinburne
he was a traitor, and he was a coward, how could he
understand his theory of women anyhow,
that Swinburne, there was a bird somewhere that rattled
as he did, boring, boring, he misunderstood
death, he was too weary—how could he call
Walt Whitman's Venus a drugged Hottentot
or Walt Whitman's Eve a drunken apple-woman
sprawling in the gutter? Walt Whitman loved
women, look how he grieved in the city deadhouse
alone with the poor dead prostitute, he called her
a house once full of passion and beauty, he called her
a dead house of love; and look how he spoke to that other,
how he made an *appointment* with her, "liberal and
lusty as nature," that's what he said; and how
he put his arm around the pimpled neck
of another as if she were a *comrade*; most,
how he praised the female form, she the gate
of the body, she the gate of the soul; some bastard
or other said he was cold, he said Walt Whitman
had too much distance, he the poet of touch,
he who wrote about love-juice, he who wrote
about lips of love and thumb of love and love
spendings and amorous pourings, he said that he
was distant, he of the swelling elate and he
who sang the song of procreation, he said
that women were only vessels to him, he said
there never was either passion *or* friendship, no woman
had ever hung her arm idly over his
shoulder and no woman died for love, her heart

pounding, not for him; but what about
the breath? And what about mad filaments
and negligent falling hands? Mostly he loved them
when they were tall and gray-haired, or he loved them
when they were flushed and uberous, he was
undissuadable; he hated the bastard,
he lay there hating—so what? so what?—Wasn't
democracy itself a *femme*, didn't they know that?
Didn't they know he wanted them as partners,
to swim and wrestle and shoot? They were comrades
too, or could be, he was thinking now
of how they fought, and he was thinking of how
he talked, how he was garrulous; but he was
clean, that was important. He thinks of the spray
at night on the ferry coming back to Camden;
he thinks of his own tenderness and he thinks
of his stubbornness, obstinancy Mrs. Stafford
called it, but most of all he thinks, even here—
wherever it is—of what the *person* is—
he had created his own person and now
he was loyal to that person. His last
good thought was how he scattered blossoms, I called them,
he said, O blossoms of my blood! O slender
leaves, you burn and sting me, it is your roots
I love, it is this death I love, I called it
exhilarating, twice now, out of my breast
the dark grass grew, I will never utter a call
only their call, put your hand in mine,
incline your face. Do you remember the body?
Do you remember lawlessness? I turned
around to face the window, that is the chair
that Wilde sat in, that is the table that Burroughs

drank his tea from, though probably not; the church
is gone, there is a huge county jail
across the way, the sweet smell of shit
from Philadelphia is gone, the soot
and smoke are gone, the ferry goes back and forth
only to the new blue-and-white aquarium,
and there is a thing called "Mickle Towers" two blocks
down, and acres of grass now and empty bottles—
that at least hasn't changed; I hiss one word
from my Phoenician, the bed is too narrow, a bird
is actually singing out there.

IX.

A drop of water
from one of my wells: I hold the drop of water
and multiply and multiply it, I prime
the pump, I plant it in the ground, water
has to be planted too, it needs the sunshine,
it needs the rain—water needs water, the gravel
I got from my river, there used to be a river,
and planted it in beds. I started with gravel—
for it is still a wonder; at some point
the water was shallow and the gravel—and sand,
for there was sand underneath the gravel, glowed
an azure pink when the sun shone and the clouds,
when there were clouds, reflected in the water
and even, it seemed, in the gravel; most of all
there was one blue reflected in the other blue
as sky and water combined, and if a shadow,
whether either bird or leaf, passed into
or through that sky it passed into or through

that water too so there was a movement of sky
and there was a movement of water, though sometimes
    the movement
was in the water itself—for there was wind too—
and then the sky was rippled by a wind
and its own shadows were deflected and more
by moving water than by clouds. There were
blossoms in that water only a month
or two ago; spring fuses suddenly with summer
below a certain line or maybe time,
after a certain point, is different—I want
to say it goes more quickly but that's too easy—
it's more erratic, sometimes it goes so slowly
you have the chance to *savor* it; I lived
with both those kinds of time, I lived so slowly
one of the years my hair was white when I
got back—I was away—and my blue hands
shook, I hardly could write, I think it was forty
years ago, I was in Scotland. It was
an agony making a choice between the cherry
and the flowering crab, just as it was agony
choosing the right kind of marble for the basin
between the honey locusts, or the right
color shirt, the blue or the white, or which kind of flower
or which kind of fruit, the fig or the apricot,
before the destruction.

X.

                    I was only fifteen
when my class went to Harmony to learn
about community; I sat on the bench where

they sang and I was suddenly lost. Half a
century later I can still hum some music
and I can still remember the blue T-shirt
I wore on the bus. That was outside Pittsburgh
where no one lived in harmony, though there was
a Scotchman there who watched us work from his perch
on one of the hills. With one of his eyes he hunted
for Christ and with the other he watched for vagrants
and drunks and lovers. I was arrested one night
for loitering, and I spent six hours in a cell
because I didn't have the dime to make a phone call;
but I believed in the future kingdom, coming
as it did from my collection of disordered sources,
the left and the right, and my religion and their religion,
and some kind of longing made up of mostly states
planted in the brain I mixed with those other states,
requiring most of all a type of innocence
and indignation—or rage—hiding itself
behind some niceness—I think that's it—it takes in
the past and the future, it mixes one with the other
and makes them the same. The bus had a long nose,
buses had long noses in those days,
and smaller wheels. The seats were large and comfortable
and not too close together and there was a heavy
smell, a mixture of gasoline and leather,
and there were long leather straps and great pockets
in back of the seats—the chairs. Men and women,
they sat on opposite sides of the center aisle
singing their songs, the words rising, they watched
for Christ, they lived *in harmony*, their houses
were comfortable, they ate five meals a day,
they worked in Socialist splendor, they believed

in celibacy, they practiced foretaste, they built
delicate birdhouses, they manufactured silk,
they grew grapes; and there were trustees, they hated
indolence, there was a sinner's bench
facing the congregation; buttons could not be
too bright, ribbons too blue. I loved
my teacher, I think his name was Wilson, he was
a good Scotchman, his fingers were yellow from smoking
Camels—or Luckies—the green had not yet gone
to war—he had a shiny forehead, his glasses
were crooked, oh I longed for someone to teach me,
to give me books, I loved the harmony that he loved,
and he knew I could have been a disciple, but he was
tired and a little demoralized. His eyes
were red behind those lenses, all those years
I wanted a teacher, here I am at the far end
of my own teaching still thinking of that, still planning
a different life, regretting my darkness, almost
pitying it. My mother only once
told the truth about her father, the saint
who sent his boys to work when they were twelve
so he could sit there reading. "He never kissed me
once," she said, "he never touched me." She was
eighty-five when she said that, she would have
eight more years; we talked at the end, we learned
to love each other.

XI.
                    Always there were two states
and endless traffic between them. I wonder what
the one pernicious thing that sings would do

if there weren't that safety valve, but it's not
just that, it's in our blood, there is an enzyme—
there is a *starch*—that forces us to go
back and forth, but I should talk who live like
the worst of them, like Africanus himself
some days, washing myself in light, driving
blurry-eyed down my highway, partly seeing
the two levels, traveling over my own head
as in a skycar, as in a 1938
Chrysler with a nose so long it turns by
itself, half-chugging its way along and even
makes decisions itself, including the backing
up, for the nose backs up, or walking through my wall,
like this, like this, or mostly climbing hills
with one hand holding on to a branch and hoping
there's a connection and hoping it's not too rotten
to hold me up and the other almost swimming—
and anywhere it wants—though I never knew
why it was needed to shudder at what we were
born loving in order to love our dying
and why we had to loathe ourselves starting with
the shoulder, say the left, say one breast,
if we had breasts, say the twisted bone
below the knee or say the chin or say
the veins, the ones in the neck, the ones in the forearms
we could have been proud of, say the liver that cleaned us,
say the voice box, say the brown lungs
or the left testicle. I have adored my body
and I have never felt disgraced though I was
shy like anyone else and I was on guard
walking naked with a number on me in
front of a row of doctors at the post office

during and after the war, wearing my glasses,
dreading each time the slippage of my two eyes,
but I was never disgusted, nor did I have to
hate the one thing in order to love the other
nor love in order to hate—that is a kind
of craziness, I hardly believe it, I wince
a little to think that great and tender men
have felt that way. And what gets purified?
And what do you think is unchangeable? But I
don't want to argue, the leaves are falling, the walnuts
are rotting on my street, the squirrels are living
in uncreated light though they would call it
something else; they eat so fast and turn
the flesh so fast they raise themselves, they are
embraced that way, they draw near and they sing
that way. And what does it mean for them to know
and not to change? And what does it mean to be
delivered? Don't you like my squirrel? Am I
too fey this way? Then what do you think of females
eating the fruit and males hiding and both
gone back to dust? And what do you think of some
with well-directed love and some still hanging
by the rear nails and one ripping up a newspaper
and carrying it into a tree, China and Bosnia
buried in its teeth, and four or five
still divided by wars and quarrels, one tree
fighting against another, some short-lived
romance, some stupid flag, and peace ignored—
and harmony—and living in wretchedness,
the future life abandoned, false hope, false happiness
abounding, misery for all, the snow

coming in early October, the newspaper soaked,
the branches icy, a terrible time to lie
in the heated nests, waiting for judgment, hearing
voices in the leaves; nor can they lie there
a thousand years—they are just squirrels—they can't
even read the book of life in the stiff newspapers
they lie in, nor is there even a fire for
them, no holocaust, nor is there a throne
or a handkerchief to wipe away their sorrows—
but since I won't convert there will not be
a Judgment—at least for now—for that depends
on me, the Jew, converting, that means Elijah
his chariot of fire, that means explaining
and arguing, for he, Elijah, he is
an expert on conversion for there is fire
in both of his lungs—since he never died—he will
expound, expound, he has read Paul, and I
will listen for I have respect for his hat—he is
a tried-and-true angel, a messenger, with a tinted
beaker, he will tie me up and read
from First Corinthians, chapter 15, the sting
of death is sin, the dead are risen, he
should know, Elijah, he was lifted, there was
a kind of wind. Ah I am contentious, I am
stubborn—what will become of me? And I am
carnal, and I am dispersed—ask Augustine!—
and bitter and benighted—ask him! He says
a body can burn and not be burned, it is
a way of supplying pain forever, he says
a diamond can only be wrought by goat's blood; he says
a lady from Carthage was healed of cancer by a single

neckbone and she is well known and care was taken
to publish only the facts; he says the reasoners
argue in vain; he says an animal of earth
even if dead can live in the sky; he says
infants will get their adult bodies and women
will not become men and fat people need not fear
that they will stay fat; he says we will know all things
with certainty, that we will draw our life
from the spirit and need no other nutriment; he says
the body will live and not be detached; he says
we cannot see as yet, that which is perfect
has not yet come—we will see with our hearts
and we will see with our future bodies for the eye
will be like the mind, as far as seeing; he says
our thoughts will all be visible; he says
our eyes will be shut but we will see, he says
we will have justice, knowledge too, he called it
"our Sabbath"—still—but needed one more day
to bring things to a close, an eighth, he says
there will be memory but no pain but we
will delight in the pain of those not there. He ends with
"end without end." He also ends with the poet's
apology, with a bow.

XII.

October twenty-third
I stood in the doorway of the African church
on Governor Street. I had a steel tape in my hand
as if I were there to measure doors and windows
or living on the river again and thinking
of the Great Shul and the final reconstruction

though truth was I was living near the railroad tracks
a block or two below the church. I sat
in my white silk armchair reading Ezekiel
and thinking of cubits. My humor was of the type
that lived on incongruities; it was
a little low but I was low myself
and angry. I was shocked by the tiny room.
There only were two benches and four or five chairs
behind the benches. It would have been an insult
to do Jerusalem, to think about cherubs and palm trees
or put a lion by the window or an eagle
of multiple parable with a shred of one thing
in one claw and a shred of other in the other,
or to describe the shining man on the stream
underneath the front steps and the trees
that grew on the left and the right or turn the table
into a true altar, with horns coming out
and troughs for blood and a place for the knife and a room
behind the cloakroom to ask forgiveness of the goat
and cleanse the spirit. There was a piano on the left
and there was a row of hymnals on a shelf
and sheet music and two or three cups and sugar.
The minister was ninety; he looked through you,
though he was mostly blind. His hair was white
and he was thin. He parked his car in front,
on the wrong side, three feet from the curb, with the end
sticking out, it was an aging Chrysler
from the days when Chevys were the size of
Cadillacs, with glitter a baby Toyota
would never aspire to—and the steps, painted green,
were much too steep, by yards and inches, a failure
of hand and eye, they were the wrong steps for that

building, even the rails were out of sync,
but I went there for several weeks to sing
and even to argue—for we did Bible study—
and fought over the meaning, that is the minister
fought with everybody. I thought he was Whitman
born a second time—I thought he would shout
about the perfect republic down the road
a thousand years or so from now but he was
biblical—and though in his sermon he brought out
everyone's sweetness—and he was funny—he railed
against the only abomination, sleeping
men with men—but it was all right, I guess,
the other abominations, father, mother,
sister, daughter's daughter, mother's sister,
mother and daughter, wife and sister, wife
of a neighbor—or a beast; and it was fine
eating fat and swallowing blood and sucking
the white flesh of a pig or the green of a snail
or forgetting salt or picking the last grape
or lying to your wife or killing or robbing
or mingling cotton and wool or using enchantment
or cutting your flesh or leaning on the scales
or cursing your mother and father or charging money
for air and water or not starving yourself
enough or burning lamps enough or wiping
the slate clean every fifty years—only fucking
and sucking counted and only birdies with birdies;
whereas Whitman, who loved to walk into churches,
he was the first to sing and he was the first
to love birdies and he was the first to love
whores and love the dried-up and sick and love
even toadies and bullies. I tried to learn

from him—I tried to listen—he believed
in a thousand cheeks and he didn't draw his love
out of what he hated, he didn't separate
the one thing from the other. I do that
too much, I have my own kind of purity
and I have horror too, and disgust. I think
I went there for the name, it was the name
of my first shul—Beth El; the door faced east—
I couldn't let that go—and it was closed
six days a week, as in Ezekiel, and there was a
roar, as in Ezekiel, only on the
street and it was cars—going north—and not a
voice singing. There was a dragonfly
who flew from the toolbox to the Last Supper
and rested on the frosted window. She was
looking for light, I guess, or food. The *basso*
profundo on my bench went crazy, he chased her
first with a prayer book, then with his bare hand,
but she was too quick. She was a visitor
from some other realm—she may have been Whitman, she may
have been the Ghost or only only my ghost,
come too far too soon; I smiled with relief
when the *basso* missed her.

XIII.
                        December fifteen Hot Dog
was lying on the sidewalk outside the Odessa
half on cement, half on the metal doors
of the cellar entrance with her head on the hip
of her friend and he was lying the other way
with his head on hers—shoes in a box—the way couples

lay in Europe for hundreds of years only they
were not in a bed but on the ground; in Europe
they lay like that because the beds were too narrow
sometimes to lie there side by side; you and
I know singles, called "twins," and doubles, called "full-size,"
and queen-size and king-size and sometimes three-quarters, all
standardized now, including sheets and blankets
and mattress covers and goose-down quilts from Lands' End
and Murphys, sofabeds, and studio couches,
and waterbeds and hot-sand-filled and motorized
and downy sleeping bags and bony futons;
but I remember odd-sized beds with strips
of steel and exposed springs and I remember
they were shorter and they were much narrower,
though where Hot Dog lay there were no springs
and it was cold and they were there without
covers, they didn't even have the sense to find
a doorway, I think they were drunk, they just fell over
and slept where they fell; I saw them at ten that night,
they could have been there for hours, they seemed almost
    peaceful,
but odd, without possessions; there was noise
around them, people were talking, there was a group
sitting on the steps beside them smoking
and drinking. I just stood there for a minute
watching, I had seen her once that morning
and once the day before, both times she had
a bottle in her left hand. I talked to her
but she was incoherent; I was struck
by how short she was—I thought she was taller—and how
beautiful she was, she wore a kerchief

with black and red squares and she had arranged it so
that she was almost pert; both times I gave her
money but it was matter-of-fact, there wasn't
pity involved, or indignation, or self-
righteousness; I waited for some dark light
to turn bright in front of the Odessa,
I wanted to *feel* the light; I did it by stages,
with one eye then the other, I almost threw
myself down on their bed, there it was,
their bluntness on that stone, their simplicity,
their helplessness. I don't know what I ought
to call it, it was a kind of altar, half
cement, half steel; I hung on to my end
of the ladder, we were wavering there, though I was
never unattached; there was some light
on their bodies—I knelt down to watch them—
more on them than anyone else, though it could
have been where they were lying; I couldn't leave them
and stayed and stayed, it would have been too cruel
to go at once, though I would see them again,
probably in the morning. I couldn't tell
whose mind they were in besides my own. I struggled
with pity first, then humor. If I had chalk,
I said to my lips, I'd draw a thick white heart
around them, that would be their Pocono bed—
I forgot *those* beds—they must be standard
too, there must be sheets and blankets to match,
in red, I guess, and white. Maybe one cry,
I said to my lips, would change it all, one roar,
one sound on the horn, just one, one silver trombone
shaking the window, maybe a cello mourning

beside them, someone playing on the sidewalk
while they slept—I said that, but look what Blake said, look
what Dickinson said. I wandered around without moving
for I was lonely and they were lonely and the smokers
and drinkers were lonely even though across the street
the park was open again, though it was closed
and locked for the night so we couldn't sneak inside
and live in tents and push our shopping carts
from place to place and live with the trees again
and rest beside the bandshell, it was warm
when we did that, we were together, though rain
and diseased skin and greedy thoughts divided us,
just as it did those across the street
and down the avenues. I bowed and kissed
my scarf, a gift from one pianist to another,
I held my feet together—we call that rocking—
and said goodbye—what else could I do?—there wasn't
even a hat to throw a dollar into,
to bend suddenly, as in a kazatsky, one leg
forward and one behind and, in one motion,
put the money onto the lining and walk
with both legs bent and both shoulders bearing
the burden; there wasn't even a bridal apron
to throw your money in and dance with the bride
one turn around the sidewalk; there was nothing
to sing for or remember.

XIV.
                    Upstairs I opened
the window and breathed some ice; I clapped my hands
and there was a burst of wings; it was the noise

of a bird taking off, it flew down to the wheelbarrow
and over the house on Ninth Street—maybe the number
would be the same except it would be even
and mine was odd; it stopped at a window—everything
stops at windows—and then it soared; the second bird
stayed on the fire escape adjusting its feathers
before it soared; it was a sudden sharp clap
for it was a dove, as I remember, and doves
are sudden and sharp and land with a splash; the third
clap she came back with a Snicker's wrapper
in her mouth and the fourth clap she was gone
forever, probably now she sits in front
of Sappora East waiting for the raw fish,
or K and K waiting for some blood soup
with sour cream inside. Goodbye ugly dove,
I loved you too much, you with your hopeless pecking,
you with your gluttony and lust. I liked
the clapping though and kept the window open
for bird after bird long long after the water
had left the fruit stores and the Polish restaurants
on First and Second Avenues. I loved
doing all that, it was good for the heart,
so was the breathing in and out, the ice
going up and down my lungs; I walked around
with the window open, I let the cold air
blow down my papers, even turn the pages
of my library books, all lying there lacerated,
with paragraphs bent and corners turned down and pencil
marks in the margin and sentences underlined
and toilet paper marking the places and coffee
stains on one or two pages, all of that,
or some of that, and one or two spines half-broken,

the way they make the books today; and opened
one of my spiral notebooks and twisted the wire
back inside the coil. I remembered
birds were meant to fly down, birds had to eat
somewhere, but I was too happy that day for bitterness,
for one of those mean asides. I was delighted
the last clap didn't come back but went foraging
somewhere out there, and there—even among
the flushed on Third Avenue, wherever plastic
was spilled or something was dropped—there was so much
I never could have seen. What I do dream
is that they come inside—what makes them so wary?
Why don't they lose their spirit? Why don't they walk
from one room to the other and come to rest
on top of the refrigerator, this being
the place of their descent and with their murmurs
destroy me, I the one who clapped them?

XV.

                                    The book
to the left of the dry daffodils is ripped
along the seam at the edge of the board. I open it
with two doves in my throat; I used to have
a foot-high statue of the bound slave,
a copy of Milton, a copy of the Bible,
a picture of my fiancée and, later,
certain rugs, and pipes, and pencils. I never
had a death's-head, not as such, and I never
had a dog, or a lion, at my feet,
and I didn't have many tools of the trade, but I
had a cushion I loved and a candlestick

and cat after cat, one that purred on my lap
and made it hard to reach my notebook, one,
believe it or not, that sat on my head, his comforter
either a watch cap or a beret, his perch
terrific for viewing. I could stare for hours
at either my grandmother Libby on one wall
or a ceramic rooster on the other, his red comb
enormous, his legs a deep orange, his tail
fluffy and stylized, more like a drawing. I
had a table once in a second cellar, almost
scooped out of the earth, the stone and wood
were covered with dust, with falling dirt, the light
coming in from a filthy casement, yet I put
a piece of Turkish rug underneath my feet
and pussy willows in a vase so I could
rub them from time to time; and when I write
in a drugstore or a restaurant I make
a small house for myself, with paper napkins
and salt faced such a way and maybe a photo
of Tolstoy or Buber or one of my love I carry
next to my wrinkled cards so I can turn
one world into another, so I can be
alone with those drugs around me or the smell
of goulash or the sounds of Hell coming through
the ceiling speakers. St. Jerome was sitting
behind a lectern working on his Bible
and there was a lion asleep on the floor and a dog
sleeping beside the lion and there was a death's-head
alone on his shelf to the right, a Slavic type
if I know types, and light pouring through the bull's-eye
windowpanes and casting delicate shadows
on the walls and mullions. Around his head

more light was pouring, it was radiant
with light for he was surrounded, yet he was
bilious, all that black bile had ruined him and changed
all his proportions, vapors had risen to his brain
and he was sluggish and suicidal yet
he wrote and wrote. I who am living now
there are no vapors in my life, I stare
a little at walls, I overreact, I am
too irritable. Though once a doctor of mind
wanted to commit me. I was suffering
from excess; he was frightened and a little
offended—he was uneasy—I thought he might faint
and hit his head on the table; I tried hugging
him but he almost jumped; he was suffering
from insufficiency, the major cause
of detached retinas. I love the lion's tail
and the cushion underneath the skull and I love
the skull for being so unadorned, for being
just wretchedly itself, at the same time being
both symbol and individual, absolute human,
almost abstract, on the one hand, and on the other
someone who once was precious, someone, some *thing*
that breathed, and moved its chest, that screamed, or even
sighed, the most touching thing we do, unless
it is to look up with our own blinking eyes
or touch something lightly with our hand, or kiss it
sweetly with our lips.

XVI.
                    The last time
in 1993 I saw her she was

sitting again on the curb. The weather was warm
for late December, there was the smell of spring
for an hour or two, belying the twenty below—
counting wind chill factor and the mind's chill—
we were expecting from the west and the north.
She had no handcuffs on, her arms weren't forced
behind her and she wasn't chained to a tree.
In fact she stretched and smiled when she saw me; I
who wanted to tell her how sorry I was, who longed
to know where she came from and know her true name and talk
about school with her and how it was she broke
away—and when—I tried to talk but we
couldn't reach each other—not that way. I almost
asked her if there was something I could do,
as if I could change my life for her—or would—
or she would know what to say. "Get out of my light"—
I wish she could have said that—"Don't stand in front of me,"
"Give me a hundred dollars," "Give me the key
to your apartment," "Give me half the stocks
you inherited when your mother died,
and whatever you do don't do it with a flourish,
remember the orders of charity, don't
let the right hand know what the left hand doesn't,
walk for ten minutes in my shoes if you
can squeeze your huge white foot inside a size
five, at least give me another dollar,
but don't watch me hide it; don't stare at me!" There were
bones in the park, they came to life all white
and red when I clapped. There were those tents. No one
had a fixed home, they walked in circles and slept
near the great bandshell, someone sat on a stone
above their heads—they all could see it, someone

sat *like* a stone, he was a stone, though sometimes
his eyes watered; the mayor sat on their faces,
the police stung them in their shoulder blades
and on the soles of their feet. People were moths,
she and I were sure of that, and the dead
turned into moths, they both had ears and elbows,
they could feel and think; although it was
a little more refined than that and there wasn't
a break between one moth and the next, the only
exception being that one was exposed, or call it
illuminated, and they were made of dew—
that was their substance, whatever it is their form was;
moreover there had to be a gate, how could you
go through without a gate? If it was locked
there wasn't much joy, but it was open and moths
hung on the crosspieces and vines covered
the uprights, some kind of trumpet, I wouldn't be
surprised if they trilled a little, although the gates
on Avenue A were made of iron and locked
after ten so we had to walk the streets
between the Odessa and Little Creatures, between
the library and the hospital. There was
a stack of bricks in front of the ancient school
at First and Ninth, the right-hand side going north,
and it was covered with plastic and held together
by steel bands. I touched it every time
I went that way, it was five feet high
and seven or eight feet long and dense and heavy
and out of place. I tried to loosen one brick
five or six times. I wanted to break the mass,
to loosen the metal and let it sing when the wind

blew under it, to let the plastic do
its whip dance but I couldn't even budge it
though I moved from place to place. Of course with shears
you could cut the metal, you could do it
with a good knife, and as you threw the bricks
the stack would spread out, it would become a pile
and then a heap. It would be good for justice,
better than stones, there is more equability;
you could say, say, twenty bricks for robbing a gas station,
all below the neck, unless a weapon
was used, or violence was done, then maybe thirty
and ten of those in the head, maybe seven in the shins
for smoking a joint, and twenty for forging a check
and ten of those in the head—at fifteen paces—
and maybe thirty minutes for murder and five
or more throwing, and thirteen paces, and no
restrictions; and going through a red light, God,
and being late with the rent and not paying
child support, and lying to the I.R.S.,
and not shoveling your walk, let alone crimes
of the heart, not being sweeter, not being kinder,
turning to stone—or brick—or fleecing or polluting
a trust; and bribery, two hundred bricks
for bribery, a hundred and one for flattery,
when money and power were at stake. Racketeering
and plundering; blackmail, encroachment, slander,
    corpse-robbing;
intimidation, conspiracy, obstruction, arson. The codes
would have to be rewritten, there would be
a new occupation, brick throwing, also hearsing,
picking up the bodies, unless the squads

were used—the legal profession would change, law schools
would study the nature of brick, courthouses
would have to be made of bricks—stone was too crude
and there is a limit to stone though not to clay,
fired as it is. And sticking pins, what is that,
assault? Is it invasion? How many bricks
for one invasion? For two? And shouting in the streets;
or mimicry; or staggering. Why didn't Nixon
sit there on the curb? And Ollie North, *prickus
americanus*, polluting his trust and wanting
our love for that; fraud, concealing, evading,
our national pastimes; baseball—and lying;
   and unctuousness,
it's called debasement; it's called slime. There was
someone else, named Coffee. Iced Tea you know,
and there was Pizza, and Clark Bar. I'm sorry about Hot Dog
but that is her name. Whatever it was before. I
hope she thinks about the curled edge
of the spotted lily. I hope her bed will be huge
and the wind will derange her hair.

XVII.

                         Historically
the thaw takes place the end of January
but sometimes as late as my birthday. It is lovely
watching the park fill up and walking over
the melted ice and putting newspapers down
on the wet benches, or sitting next to someone
drinking a cup of coffee and letting sleep
almost take over again. The woman on my left

wore black leg warmers and a yellow slicker.
She had a band on her head to keep her ears warm
and hold her hair in place. She wore sneakers—
size six it looked like—they were so wide
they were like hooves. The man on my right had a beard
and wore a loose-fitting suit and a heavy overcoat—
and boots—and he was bareheaded. One of them
was only a soul, I knew that, but I didn't
know which. The woman kept her hands in her pockets
and her legs were stretched out; the man was mumbling, he
would be the hard one to reach. My back faced the street
so I was facing the playground; we were drinking
our morning coffee but there was a little Old Crow
and a little Schenley and just enough smoke; I clapped
my hands, it wasn't a great explosion, only
a tap; for all my neighbors knew it could have
been a *thought*, a little extension, and there was
some color under my feet, a tiny pool
of water and a shred of ice, a muted
oily rainbow. I splashed my shoe and spread
the colors out, some greens and some reds; it was
a good day for belief. "Never again," I said
to the water; you will never drown me
no matter what; this colored puddle will be
my token for that, and "never again" I echoed,
though I was thinking about the other puddle
the second time, and I was not exactly crying,
though breathing a little hard, a ventilation
we have in our family through the female side
passed on through the oldest male and I was the oldest—
and I felt very old—though truth was I was

the youngest too, my own riddle, and I
felt young today, what with the rain what with
the wind what with a rolling bottle that won't
let me alone and yesterday morning's news
still underfoot and all those trees still bare
but starting to turn a little and two or three birdlets
getting ready again for the next eternity.